W^{My}exford

The Raven Point

By Anne Rossiter

The morning sun caresses the Raven Point
Waves lap their hypnotic rhythm
In this haven of quiet solitude.
On sands unmarked by human foot,
Only the seabirds leave prints,
Like hieroglyphs on virgin sand.

Shells, numerous as my thoughts, decorate the shore.
Crabs, victims of the tide, will never crawl to maturity.
The winds of time will erase the evidence of their brief existence,
Helped by the predators of the seashore.
I stand and watch and am helpless.

On the horizon a ship sails,
Perhaps to some exotic port.
The shimmering waves carry her effortlessly
Out of sight, out of mind, out of time.

Warm sun penetrates my body.
Heart and waves beat in unison.
My soul is at peace,
In this place of perfect solitude.

The Raven Point or as locals call it 'The Point of the Raven' is one of my favourite places in My Wexford. It combines sea, sand, forest, wildlife and walking paths. Much of the evergreen forestation is relatively new having been planted as dune reclamation after the reclamation of the North Sloblands. The spit of sand that was the original point of the raven formed an arm enclosing Wexford Harbour from the north and almost joining the burrow of Rosslare from the south.

My Wexford

Nicky Rossiter

NONSUCH

To Anne

First published 2006

Nonsuch Publishing
73 Lower Leeson Street
Dublin 2, Ireland
www.nonsuchireland.com
www.nonsuch-publishing.com

British Library Cataloguing in Publication Data.
A catalogue record for this book is available from the British Library.

ISBN 1 84588 556 2
ISBN-13 (from January 2007) 978 1 84588 556 4

Typesetting and origination by Tempus Publishing Limited
Printed in Great Britain

Contents

Introduction

My Wexford is a book about the town where I was 'born and reared'. I hope the items included will inform you. I hope they will also amuse and entertain you. Most of all I hope this book will kindle a spark of reminiscences about not just my town but about yours whether that is Wexford or any other.

I have combined personal recollections of the town in the past half-century with items going further back. The latter pieces concern events or people that give Wexford its unique character and also shed light on the ordinary lives of our forefathers.

While some of the recollections are personal, the minutiae of everyday life will be familiar to most readers. In particular I hope you will recall the comics and sweets of times past and maybe even relive those 'always sunny' summers.

The tale of murder in the Bullring is taken from contemporary newspaper records and I include it to show not just the crime but the explicit manner of reporting that was common a century ago. The residence of the victim also connects it to my personal Wexford.

As ever I include a selection of photographs. Some are from my personal collection, others were kindly provided by the owners and are acknowledged in the captions and others, given without acknowledgement, are of – as yet - unknown origin.

Any book of history depends to a great extent on the generosity of people other than the author with photographs, information and background. For this book I am eternally grateful to Sylvia O'Connor, Celestine Rafferty, Wexford County Library Service, The National Library of Ireland, Paddy Foley, Jim Billington, Nicky Rossiter (senior), Marie O'Byrne, previous co-authors and researchers and many others. Without Eoin Purcell and Nonsuch Publishing these words would still be languishing on the hard drive.

Of course no book, article or radio script would be possible without the support and encouragement of my wife Anne, who also provided the poem *The Raven Point*, plus Mark, Daithi, Kate, Paula, Elli, Fin…….

I

The Street

The experiences of the resident of one street is not unique to that location or person, so I am sure people from other streets and different towns will find echoes of their past in this chapter.

Up until relatively recently the street of Bishopswater was referred to on the register of electors as New Houses, Distillery Road. This is typically Wexford in its attitude to change. The estate of 127 houses at Bishopswater was built in 1951. Prior to that I am told – I was too young to remember – I lived on Clifford Terrace. I am also led to believe that when I lived there my cot was the bottom drawer of a wardrobe. After all, it was a time when newly weds and even young families did not have their own house of flat to live in and most commonly rented a room in a family house.

Wexford Corporation built Bishopswater on land opposite Alvina Brook, a Pierce development of a few years earlier. The name of the estate probably comes from the river running behind Alvina Brook. In genteel society this was known as the Bishopswater River but to us it was always the Horse River. One assumes that some bishop had land at Ballinagee, where the river rises, in the dim and distant past. Then again it might be a fanciful name dreamed up by the distillery marketing team or whatever such people were called in the 1800s.

In speaking about the street we will be looking at it holistically. For us the street was the 'front of Bishopswater', Alvina Brook and later Casement Terrace. We refer to the 'front' to distinguish it from 'the back houses'. In fact in many ways Bishopswater had three distinct sections as far as young people were concerned. These were usually decided based on where you drew your pals. There was the section from number one to twenty four; this was where the road going to the 'back' area intersected. From number twenty-five to around forty-five continued up the main road. The 'back houses' were a self-contained circle of houses around a green area with a spur shooting off to the right ending in a cul-de-sac.

Bishopswater was a Corporation estate but thinking back to the residents there in the 1950s and 1960s it is interesting to recall the occupations of the people and note

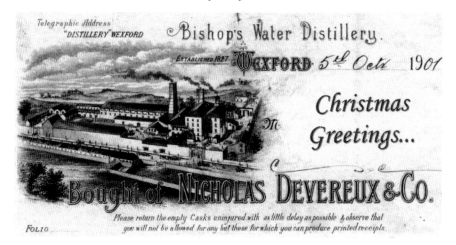

The Bishopswater Distillery: This is a beautiful reproduction of one of the billheads of the distillery dating from 1901 that was used as a Christmas card by Wexford Library service. Note the structure of the name – Bishop's Water Distillery. See also the warning about returning casks. The sketch accurately reproduces the distillery and surrounding houses. The entrance at the bottom of today's Casa Rio is exactly the same. The houses of old Maudlintown are depicted and the vast extent of the complex is brought to life. (Wexford Library Collection)

how diverse they were for local authority housing. Between just numbers 1 and 24 there was a person who built a grocery shop beside his house; there was a member of An Garda Siochana, a lighthouse keeper, a lightship crewmember, a lorry driver, post office workers, foundry workers and a Department of Agricultural inspector among many others. Such a diversity of families made life in Bishopswater a great experience and gave us a wide range of views and activities

As stated above, we unofficially incorporated Alvina Brook into our street by drawing our friends from those houses. Pierce's built Alvina Brook and the majority of the residents worked in the foundry; usually they were foremen in various departments – my grandfather more commonly called 'The Da' was the forge foreman while Paddy Quirke was in charge of the electricians. Alvina Brook was unusual in a number of ways. It had and still has lovely redbrick faced porches at the front door. Inside they were unique in that all internal doors were originally sliding doors. One other point is that the house numbers went up to 12 but there were only ten houses, numbers 1 & 2 were not used. To add to the confusion numbers 3 & 4 were not let directly to Pierce's employees. O'Connors in number 3 had a huge side garden adjoining The Knock.

Willie Goodison lived at number 1 Bishopswater and he developed a thriving and ever expanding retail business on some land beside his house. The abiding memory of that land after his first shop was built was that it was 'yella marl'. This was wet, sticky and yes yellow in colour and many a Wellington boot was sucked from a foot as we trudged around in the pools of water that gathered there.

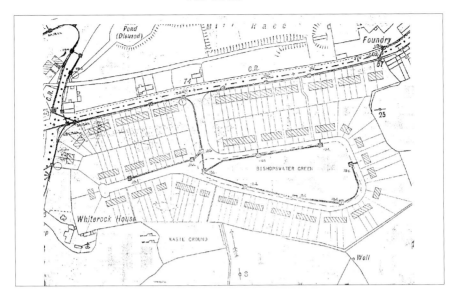

Bishopswater: This old map shows Bishopswater as it was laid out in 1951. The foundry in the top right was where we had the garage beside Casa Rio. The Millrace was long gone by the time we used The Knock. Look at the size of the gardens on offer in local authority housing backing on to Whiterock House. (Rossiter Collection)

Goodison's shop epitomised much of the retail quirks and services of the 1950s and 1960s. Those were the days of choice despite scarce financial resources. You could buy all varieties of 'broken biscuits' at a reduced price – presumably the better off customers did not like to serve such fractured fancies for tea. This was the period of the tins of biscuits arrayed around the counter of such shops. In later years they were fitted with glass lids to view before you opened. The customer went round with the paper bag – plastic bags were well into the future – selected a few of each variety and brought them to the shop assistant to weigh and charge. Sweets were also sold loose in those days and 'five a penny' or 'ten a penny' were the usual choices. There were also the specials such as penny toffee bars or lucky lumps or 'peggie's legs' that were only purchased at special days of the week. We earned our pennies by 'doing the messages'. Cooked ham, luncheon sausage and corned beef were sliced on the premises using a lethal looking electric machine. People usually purchased this cold meat by the number of slices required rather than the weight. We watched fascinated as the assistant sliced the meat – were we waiting for a bit of finger to go into the mix?

During the week it was common to be sent down to the shop with a list of necessities written on a scrap of paper and the note on the bottom to 'put it on the book'. This was an informal credit system that most local shops operated with the bill being paid off on Friday, which was the normal payday. I suppose some small interest was charged because more often than not if you were sent down with a few quid to clear the bill on Friday night you got a lollipop or a few sweets from Willie.

Goodison's was the location of the public telephone before a kiosk was provided – many years later. Ironically the public telephone was far from public. You
went to the shop and asked to use the telephone and you were directed into the
garage – a storeroom really – where the old telephone with the A and B buttons was on the wall. You put the money for the call in the slot and dialled. If it
was answered you pressed button A. If there was no reply you pressed B and the
money was refunded. Remember the days of going into telephone boxes and
pushing button B just in case someone had forgotten to claim their refund?

In later years Willie added petrol pumps and then built a pub at the side of the
shop.
Sometimes we got odd jobs from Willie. You might get to deliver some groceries
to an older resident, be tidying up the garage, burning rubbish out the back or
over in the Knock. Some were even allowed to serve petrol. Another thing about
Goodisons was they had perhaps the first German Shepard or Alsatian on the
road. Rusty or Rinty was the name.

At the top of the road Browne's shop was a different matter and always seemed
a bit more 'posh'. Funnily enough this was my first place of employment in the
shop and pub back in the mid 1960s. My main memories are slicing meat on the
whirring electric slicer, stacking the pub shelves and working with Sean Flynn
and Miriam Donohoe. At one time our neighbours Anna and Har Peare opened
a little shop in their front parlour.

One memory of Goodison's has nothing to do with the shop. They were the
first family to have not only a television but also one with a BBC aerial; you
know the big H shaped one. When Cassius Clay fought Sonny Liston their front
room was packed with adults and children to watch the spectacle in flickering
black and white.

Another long gone memory associated with Bishopswater relates to the men
who worked on the lightships. These fathers of our friends were gone from the
street for a month and then home for a few weeks then gone another month. The
iconic reference to these lightship men was 'the basket'. Living for a month on a
trawler size boat out in the sea meant taking all your provisions with you. These
were packed into big canvas covered wicker baskets that were collected by horse
and cart at regular intervals and transported to the ship.

Cars were few and far between back in the 1960s in Bishopswater. Mr Lenihan
owned one. He was an agricultural inspector and needed transport for his job
but I recall that even in those days of little or no traffic he often parked the car in
The Knock. He was always popular when he transported us to school in George's
Street on a wet morning.

The lack of cars was very evident in the fact that despite having the natural
playground of The Knock we spent much time and energy playing on the road
that was the main artery coming into Wexford from the south west of the county.
The street games of choice were hurling – it was the glory days of Wexford

hurling –, Scotch, Chase or tig as we called tag. The hurling needs no explanation but how many remember Scotch?

All you needed was a small ball – preferably not too hard – and a gang of wild children. The game started with all participants bar one lining up with feet wide apart and their backs to the starter. He or she (it was a multi-gender game) bowled the ball between the legs of one person. That person had to chase and pick up the ball. The aim then was to hit other participants with the ball. When hit you were out. Someone else grabbed the ball and on it went. I think there was a rule that if a person caught the thrown ball before it hit or landed the thrower was out. The last person with the ball started the next round. Don't tell anyone but during such games as with chase and tig the children of Bishopswater had little respect for private property with hedges being jumped over and through, gardens hidden in and not a few cars hit by the ball.

Not that all games took place on the street. A certain elite – who shall remain nameless – had a very sophisticated game called 'army'. This was in the days when we were less politically correct with regard to toy guns and glorifying violence. The 'commander' even went to great lengths in cutting out and colouring 'stripes' for members being promoted to corporal or sergeant. Part of the initiation or promotion process included being locked in a dark garden shed for a period – usually after hearing tales of rats or mice. It might also require and expedition down the tunnel of the Horse River or performing a task devised by the 'commander'. Although most families cultivated the back gardens some did not. In one such uncultivated garden 'the army' dug an underground bunker. This was hard work. It was about four feet deep by seven or eight feet square and topped with timber planks covered with soil and had a narrow entrance gap.

Recalling those army days reminds me of the fact that like in the nursery rhyme, people once did use vinegar and brown paper for curing headaches. In those days we did not have designer runners, if you wore such footwear they were those horrible flat plimsolls, so most days we went around in proper leather shoes. These usually had leather soles with possibly big metal tacks in the heel edges to reduce wear. On one occasion I remember running through a friends back yard in such shoes. I hit an area with pebbles embedded in the concrete and went slap on the ground headfirst. The ensuing headache was massive but I was one of those youngsters who would not take tablets. The alternative was a Mrs Cullen's or a Beecham's powder. These were diabolical painkillers in powder form that came in little folded papers. The former had a green label and the latter had brown bits in among the white granules. I remember people emptying these powders onto their tongues and then washing it down with water. No way was I doing that so I spent the afternoon lying on the sofa with that light brown – almost tissue – paper that grocers wrapped your bread in soaked in vinegar on my forehead. I do not recall if it worked but I didn't take the pills or powders. Another home remedy I remember was when I hade a ferocious stomach-ache one night. My granny gave me a sip of brandy to ease it and either it worked or I was drunk on the sip.

Alvina Brook: This shot of Alvina Brook shows the old 'garage' in The Knock but it also seems to have a sort of round tower visible in the right hand corner. I cannot find any information on this. Another anomaly is that the houses seem to start at number 7 although the walls and gates of the other lower numbers are visible. The grass verge visible at the bottom right indicates that Bishopswater houses had yet to be built. (Rossiter Collection)

In those now far off days, Bishopswater was almost in the country. We entered into the spirit by purchasing 'day old chics' from a seller in the Bullring. We brought them home in a shoebox with holes in the lid. The dream was fresh eggs for breakfast on tap. I do not recall them dying but neither do I remember a fully-grown chicken in our garden.

What our garden did produce was a great crop of rhubarb. When planted we put old galvanised buckets upturned over the plants called stools. At times we got stalks of rhubarb that were two feet long and about six inches in circumference. Must of it was destined for tarts or to go with custard after Sunday dinner but we didn't always wait. On many sunny afternoons I remember chopping a stalk, discarding the leaf, which I seem to recall was supposed to be poison and chopping the rhubarb into half-inch pieces. These went into a bowl with a massive amount of sugar and we had a feast to eat in the open air.

Our garden had a bird shed. This was not the pigeon loft more common in estates but an area where birds – canaries and budgies – were reared and became stars of shows and sold on. They were reared from eggs and I recall my father being very worried if thunder approached while the eggs were being hatched. Those were days when many parlours boasted a yellow canary or one of those green speckled budgies called Joey. Do you remember the budgies? They had every comfort from ladders to mirrors with bells on them and bits of cuttlefish stuck through the bars. Then there were the special water fountains where we saw gravity at work without knowing it and seed containers that clipped on to the special break in the bars. Some of these had a little door to restrict feeding if necessary. A number of shops made good money on birdseed that was sold loose by the pound in brown paper bags. Later we used to be sent for special budgie seed in printed packs. The cage was covered with a cloth or newspaper to let Joey sleep because apparently he did not sleep with the light on. Children and adults spent many an hour teaching budgies to 'talk'. The biggest excitement in owning a budgie was when it escaped. This usually happened when people were cleaning out the cage. Most people did this in a closed room so they only had to spend a few hours chasing the bird around to get it caged again. Others were foolish enough to undertake the task with a window open – then it was unlikely Joey would ever return despite a handwritten advert in the local shop. Budgies could be nasty little pets – those hooked beaks were semi-lethal weapons.

Meanwhile back in the bird shed the fanciers, as the breeders were called, experimented in cross breeding worthy of a Darwinian scientist. I remember my father being particularly adept at breeding red canaries. This was generally achieved through diet and the birds were actually more orange than red. Canary rearing was almost a fulltime occupation with bird shows taking place throughout the country. Birds were shown in specially designed and painted cages for best effect. Most fanciers built the cages from plans, so that was part of the enthusiasm. I recall that

Day Old Chicks: Here we have two budding poultry keepers of the 1960s with the day-old chicks bought at The Bullring. (Rossiter Collection)

light blue was a common internal cage colour with a black exterior. Because the shows happened all over the place the birds were transported by rail – a time when there were many more stations. To facilitate this the design and construction went a step further. My father and many others made boxes or crates into which a given number of show cages fitted snugly. These were like steamer trunks with metal handles, hasps and locks. They were usually painted black with the name and address of the fancier stencilled in the lid. The crates were carried to the railway station – usually by hand – and would be met at the destination railway station by the show organisers. People with a single bird to show often transported them strapped to the back carrier of the pushbike – in a cage of course.

Bikes were the main mode of transport at that time. I don't know where the workers in Pierce's managed to store theirs or how they recognised their own bike at dinner or teatime – all bikes were black at the time. On the street bicycles were not too common among the younger generation but most learned to cycle using the father's bike. This in itself was a feat of contortion. Most of us were not tall enough to straddle those 'high Nellies' and still reach the pedals. The delineation between ladies and gents bicycles was the crossbar. I often wonder why they bothered with the two types. The only practical value was that you could carry a passenger on the bar. Back to the cycling lessons. Somehow people managed to learn to cycle by putting a leg under the bar and cycling around with the body angled out from the frame. The bicycle of the 1950s was not a leisure machine. It took people to and from work or it was the carthorse for bringing the shopping home. Almost every ladies bike had a wicker basket on the handlebars with a spring loaded carried on the back. There was also the little satchel attached to the saddle containing the puncture repair kit.

Build your Own: The advert says it all. Why was the ladies model 4/= extra? (Rossiter Collection)

The Emergency: Like so many young men, my father was a member of the LDF or Local Defence Force during The Emergency. This was the forerunner of the FCA. (Rossiter Collection)

Getting back to the street and the back gardens in particular. Every house had a shed usually referred to as the coal shed. In here depending on the interests of the man of the house could be anything and everything. One item I recall in particular was a bayonet. This was a relic of The Emergency and was kept on a small loft in the shed.

As usual we were not supposed to use it but what was going to keep a group of young lads from regularly taking it down, sliding it from its sheath and imagining all manner of death and destruction. Another thing that graced most sheds of the era was the 'last'. This odd shaped piece of iron with various shapes was the implement on which shoes were mended. Most men had a rudimentary knowledge of shoe repair to varying degrees. At the time shoes were major expenditure items and were far from disposable. Most people only had one good pair so repairs at home were essential. Leather for the soles and heels was sold in rectangular sheets in hardware shops. Can you recall that light brown sheet? If repair was needed the person laid the old shoe down on a piece of paper and traced the shape and size. This was cut out with a scissors and the shape drawn on the leather. Then the knife came out. For the semi-professional this was a hook blade affair but the more common implement was an old butter knife that had been honed and sharpened to half its normal size. Most homes had a whetstone that was used for this and for sharpening garden shears or clippers as we called them. I remember that my father had made a wooden box with a lid to hold the whetstone that was about a foot long by four inches wide with a rough and a finer side. With the sole or heel cut to shape, the old shoe was put on the last and the old leather removed.

A Day at the Races: As if to show that it was not always sunny in the past, this picture taken at the races in Bettyville dates from the late 1950s. This is noticeable from the fashions of long topcoats, caps and the Clarke's sandals. Note also the old lorry and the rather primitive marquee. (Rossiter Collection)

The new leather was tacked on with little nails called 'sparbles' and then nailed all round secure to the upper. The worker then felt round the inside of the shoe for any of these sharp points that were likely to prick the feet. When satisfied with the result he got out the heelball. This was a stick of a sort of wax material that was heated and rubbed along the edge of the leather. It came in colours to correspond with the upper of the shoes and it was used to shade the edge of the new leather to the proper colour. If someone had a tendency to wear down part of the heel excessively you would get special studs hammered into the vulnerable area. These came on a card and had three or five prongs that were hammered into the leather. They were great noisemakers but also lethal for causing people to slip.

In the early years of Bishopswater there was a wonderful piece of waste ground between Alvina Brook and Browne's pub. There were the remains of two old white washed mud wall cottages on the land and these were magnets for the children of the area. The waste ground, covered in brambles, also gave easy access to the Horse River. Here we played, splashed and fell in for most days of the summer. We put blocks and rocks across the stream to build a dam, which we strengthened with sods. Other times we threw sheets of galvanized metal across the flow and jumped on to them to cause mini tsunamis to try to drench bystanders. In dry time the flow in the river might reduce to a trickle while in winter it was a raging torrent overflowing banks six feet high in places. In between, its most common dimension was – just wide enough to leap across. At such times the river in that

Going Away: This was a typical scene at the railway station in decades past. The bride and groom along with guests usually proceeded from the wedding breakfast to the station to begin the honeymoon journey. Destinations were more likely Bray or Dublin than Dubai or the USA. (Rossiter Collection)

A wedding group sitting down to the meal in The County Hotel. (Rossiter Collection)

A Typical Family Snap: This picture was taken in the front garden at Bishopswater. Alvina Brook is in the background. The group consists of my mother, aunt and grandmother – Me Ma, Aunt Marie and the Granny. (Rossiter Collection)

area flowed over a concrete bed and usually had a build up of slimy algae. It was in jumping this type of stream we usually had an early bath. Hit the edge just wrong, out goes the foot and down we slapped on our behind in the cold water. It sounds like fun now but you consider waddling home in that wet slimy trousers when one didn't have a huge wardrobe of designer jeans to change into and the mammy ready to give you a good going over. Those were the pre-politically correct days too when the wooden spoon did more than stir the soup.

The further upriver you went the deeper it got. I had a friend who lived above Browne's crossroads in what we in our innocence would almost call a farm at the time. They had a huge expanse of ground around the house where they cultivated vegetables and potatoes. They also had apple and pear trees and blackcurrant and gooseberry bushes in abundance. In fact we were so blasé about the fruit that it was commonly used as ammunition in our mini wars among the trees. The pears were those typically Irish varieties, small and very hard. The family also kept a few pigs in a sty out the back and as part of their bedding they stored wood shavings in a shed. Thinking back it is a miracle we were not suffocated as we played in that shed hiding ourselves under the shavings. In those days the house had no piped water so they had to use a well down the bottom of the garden. To reach the well you went down a clay path along the garden – mud in winter – opened a gate and crossed a wonderful concrete bridge about two feet wide over the Horse River at a point where it ran about three feet deep. The well pipe protruded from the opposite bank. Although we didn't appreciate it at the time that was a lovely spot with trees overhanging the deep slow river with sun shining through.

That river loomed large in the lives of Bishopswater youth. One way it managed to do so was with rats. Ironically we spent our days playing in areas that were probably kingdoms of rats from riverbanks to the Pierce's scrap metal dump in the knock or traipsing down the tunnel. When rats invaded the gardens and yard of Alvina Brook it was another matter. Now we were afraid of them. My grandparents lived opposite our house at number 10 Alvina Brook. At their house you descended a flight of about ten stone steps to the yard, shed and garden. One notable thing about those sheds was that they had a window exactly like a house window with sash opening and a lock. The garden was at least twenty feet above the riverbed with a wall to keep us from falling over. In spite of this the rats occasionally burrowed up and appeared in the garden or yard. Then it was time to set the traps. These were sometimes like the mantraps or bear traps we saw in the films. On other occasions people used wire cage type traps. Slug guns, as we called pellet guns, were also used to keep the population down. Some people had rifle versions while others had pistols. I mention these because on one occasion a neighbour caught a rat in one of the snap type traps but it was still alive. To ease the suffering she decided to shoot it with her son's slug gun. This was better in thought than practice and she was found repeatedly shooting the rat in the rear end.

The other way the Horse River impinged on Bishopswater was when it overflowed in winter floods. This did not happen too often but when it did it was a force to be reckoned with. In fact at such times it joined forces with other water flows. After prolonged torrential rain the river sometimes rose high enough to flow over the back walls of Alvina Brook. At the same time run off from Whiterock Hill and from the land later developed as Wexford Golf Course flowed like rivers down the roads. At times there was a single river of water from footpath to footpath with manhole covers lifting under the pressure.

Such was my street – like a thousand other streets – with its characters, stories and fun.

II
The Weekend

FRIDAY

Weekends are always special and when looking back to the past they acquire almost magical properties.

My recollections of weekends begins with teatime on Friday. For as long as I can remember the special treat at that meal was a 'cut'. The more sophisticated call them Chester cakes but to us they were simply 'cuts'. Apparently these big thick square cakes were made from left over ingredients. Their modern counterparts are seldom as huge as ours and that is not because of childhood exaggeration. There was almost a meal in those cakes.

After tea there was another Friday ritual.

My Granda Walsh lived on Roche's Terrace, where my mother had been born, and a visit to his house was a part of my weekend. Roche's Terrace is one of three terraces of houses in Wexford that are built without any direct road frontage. With Rose Rock and Clifford terraces it is built on a height above the road with steps leading up at each end. Roche's Terrace is the highest of the three being about ten feet above Roche's Road. When I used to visit there were narrow steps on the north end and long steps on the south end. The latter has been adapted to a ramp.

So why did I go to 'The Terrace' as we called it on a Friday night, summer or winter? The answer is a combination of many things.

Of course there was a visit to the Granda. He originally came from Castlebridge and went out there every weekend, so it was important to get there early. Looking back I have no clear recollection of how he got to Castlebridge. He did not have a car so I suppose he must have cycled out via the old bridge at Carcur.

He worked in the goods yard at the North Railway Station and that reminds me of the days when most goods arrived in Wexford by rail. This was after the days when our main supply line was by sea and before the arrival of the juggernaut road transport. The goods yard was a hive of activity in those days with all manner of merchandise being delivered and stored there. A remnant of the trade is still visible in the Lyons Tea shed on the land there. The goods were either collected by local merchants or delivered by the CIE staff. Into the late 1960s that delivery was by horse and cart. Joe Breen drove the long cart with the big carthorse if the memory serves properly. Many people will recall seeing that fabulous sight that we never realised as being so great on the narrow streets of Wexford.

Thinking of those deliveries from the station reminds me of one of the most tragic accidents of the time. Access to the goods yard was obtained by crossing the tracks and hordes of messenger boys and merchants would have traversed them weekly. Then one day word spread through the town, Mr Pierce of S & R Pierce was entering or leaving the yard when a train struck his car and the poor man was killed.

Speaking of death I remember years later when Granda Walsh died. His funeral was held on the day that we heard that Nelson's Pillar was blown up. Funerals from Bride Street Church at the time went along the quay having proceeded down Bride Street to 'Coffin Corner', South Main Street and King Street and as a young person I was mightily impressed to see a train stop on the quay as the hearse passed.

But back to happier times and Friday on the terrace, the Granda was usually shaving in a tin basin in the 'kitchen' when I arrived. By way of explanation of our houses at the time I would remind you that what we call a dining room was then the kitchen. The modern kitchen was known as the 'back kitchen' and our sitting room was the parlour. At the time there was no bathroom and the toilet was outside in a galvanised shed in the yard. From the yard steps led up to a long narrow garden that was just about level with the upstairs bedrooms.

The back garden at Roche's Terrace in the 1940s. (Rossiter Collection)

My abiding memory of those visits is the aroma of hot water, soap and chips. Oh and of course the big chunky English three-penny bit I got from the Granda.

No I didn't just go there for the money, well at least not for that money. My mother, like dozens of other women of the time, ran a 'club'. This was a sort of hybrid savings club, thrift fund and credit union. The way it worked was that a number of people 'joined the club'. They agreed to pay a certain amount each week for a 'turn'. I think at the time each 'turn' cost five shillings. When everyone had joined and decided how many turns they wanted the names were put in a hat and a draw was made. Each turn was allocated a date and the person was informed with a little written slip of their pay out date. There might then be some 'horse trading' as they manoeuvred to have the pay out on a date to suit a particular need like a birthday, anniversary, wedding etc. The way the finances worked was that if twenty people joined there were 21 turns allocated with the organiser getting the 'free turn' for her trouble. Then each week the money was collected for each turn and if it was your turn you got the full amount collected, for instance in this example five pounds. In effect you paid the cost of one turn to cover administration.

Collecting this money was part of my Friday night trip back to the ancestral terrace. My aunt Peggy lived with the Granda along with her children and she was a member of the club so I collected her money.

Next door lived the Healys. They were cousins of ours I believe; as usual in Wexford almost every family is in some way related to every other – at least in the older families. Paddy Healy was a cobbler in a time when shoe repair was big business and not suffering from the disposable age. His shop was in Cornmarket and the sign is still to be seen in some old photographs. Aunt Bessie lived with Paddy and Mag Healy and their family. She was a Crosbie and was related to the Crosbies of show business and 'School Around the Corner' fame – Paddy in the latter and Martin who was a renowned singer. Both were frequent visitors to Wexford and the terrace, especially when Martin performed in the many variety shows that punctuated life in the middle of the twentieth century. Mag and Bessie were members of the club so I visited them.

Another of the Crosbie clan lived a few doors up on the terrace. She was Maggie Bergin and although she ran her own club she was also a member of this one. It was quite common to have more than one 'iron in the fire'. Some other families on Roche's Terrace were also members of the club but usually Peggy had collected their money so I did not call to them.

One other job that I loved regarding the club was the delivery of the money to the person whose turn it was. This usually resulted in a tip of a few pence and pennies bought lots in those days. Then with a pocket full of half crowns it was time to leave the terrace but the mission was not complete yet.

Another ritual of Friday night was chips and for different areas of residence or roots in the town that meant different chippers. For us it was Nellie Wrights in

Bride Street. Mrs Wright was a low sized and rather stout lady. She had a cheerful manner and an English accent. Mr Wright seldom appeared in the chip shop – we seldom used the name chipper – but Gordon ably assisted Nellie by taking care of cooking while she dished up the food. Gordon was another person with an English accent and a great manner. The 'piece de resistance' in Nellie Wrights was the rissole. Wexford people still swear that no one ever replicated the magnificent recipe although some came close. Of course there were also the fish and chips and mushy peas. There were no burgers, chilli sauce or curry in those days.

In the pocket not containing the club money I had the few bob wrapped in the note detailing the food required for us or my grandparents in Alvina Brook or some of the neighbours. These were read out to Mrs Wright and we had the orders wrapped separately in newspaper – not the plain newsprint of later times. We usually bought a bag of chips to eat on the way home. These tasted extra special on cold frosty nights as we headed back up Distillery Road. The long reign of Nellie Wrights ended tragically when Gordon died as a result of a fire on the premises.

SATURDAY MORNING

Saturday was 'messages day'. Each Saturday morning at around ten o'clock we set off for town – that's what we said when we were heading for the shopping area.

The primary mission was to pay the weekly sums on items bought 'on the book' in various establishments. This was the form of credit available to people before the credit cards, finance companies and bank accounts for all. The shops apparently financed this credit directly.

The first port of call was Coffey's. There we queued with many others at the office with our little red covered notebook and ten bob note to pay off the suit or shoes or other items purchased a few months earlier.

Another popular office on the Saturday morning was in Jenkins, our very own department store. Their office was in the upstairs area and was presided over by Sammy Coe for many years. In fact almost every store of any size or selling goods of high cost had a 'book' system. There must have been great profit even in the sale of those red notebooks because they were the most common item of commerce. As television came to Ireland another venue was added. Almost everyone rented his or her television in those days and for us that meant a weekly trip to RTV. Televisions were much less reliable in those early days and renting gave you the added comfort of an engineer on call if you had problems. Mind you it often seemed to take ages for the engineer to come out on a call. They were more in demand than doctors for house calls at the time.

The messages also involved some purchasing and Jack Fane's was one of our objectives on the Saturday mission. Fane's just south of The Bullring was one of

Jack Fane: This was one on the ports of call for the messages each Saturday morning. (Rossiter Collection)

those old Irish institutions of a pub cum grocery store. It even had a lovely little snug inside the front door. This was where the ladies had their tipple in the days before the 'lounge bar' culture took hold. Jack was a legendary GAA personality and had a huge clientele for both ends of the trade. I hasten to add that it was groceries we purchased there especially Lyons Green Label tea. Another fascination for us in Fane's was the goods elevator just inside the front door. This must have been a major leap forward thinking back to 1950s Ireland. It gave access to the cellar where the porter and other goods were stored. He probably bottled his own stout at the time, as did most publicans. They even had their own labels.

Another grocery and pub combination we had to call to was Harry Stones – where the Book Centre now stands. The messages to be collected here were usually for the Granny Rossiter and were most often from the meat counter that was located way down the shop.

While doing this the pennies collected the night before were burning holes in our pockets. George Bridges down in Selskar was mostly the attraction on special occasions when we had more than a few pennies. Favourites down there were Dinky cars, cap guns and of course the 'ammo' or rolls of caps.

A regular port of call on the Saturday morning was Woolworth's. From the ice cream cone machine at the entrance – plain, 99 or with syrup or 'hundreds and thousands' - down each aisle and out the opposite door this was a cave of wonder. No shop had such a variety of goods. Remember we were in an era of small sweet or grocery shops and a few family owned department stores but the latter specialised in clothes. For us clothes were a necessity, a chore and something best left to the mammy. We could spend hours in Woolworth's and never spend a penny. In fact for clothes shopping we usually used the 'approbation method' where a few items were brought home and tried on and the items not purchased were returned to the shop.

Across the road from Woolworth's was Buckland's and for us it could have been spelt Booklands. This is where we bought our weekly comics and if we were feeling flush we got the *Classics Illustrated* or a *Dell* comic – more on these in a different chapter.

After all those messages it was back up Distillery Road for the dinner. Yes dinner was at that time of day; lunch was what you brought to school.

SATURDAY AFTERNOON

This was our best ever part of the weekend. After the dinner it was time for the pictures or cinema as the posh people called this.

First there was the money to be procured. The pennies from last night were gone on the comics so we scrounged around. The Ma or Da or Granny or Granda usually coughed up maybe just for the joy of getting rid of us for a few hours. If you came from a larger family it was more difficult so a bit bargaining or bawling or sulking might be required.

In Wexford of the 1950s and 1960s we were spoiled for choice. We had three cinemas competing for our attention. The Abbey was the newest and usually had first run films but it was also the dearest and the furthest from Bishopswater. The Capitol had relatively new films and was closest to us but the Palace Cinema known in best Wexford tradition as the Cinema Palace was the cheapest and our favourite although they all got a good deal of our money.

I will give a quick recollection of the main points of the first two before we get to the Palace. In the Abbey you could queue under a sort of canopy – if you were going to the dearer seats. For the 'scratch' you queued down a sort of laneway. The Abbey had a big shop directly in front of the entrance although most people stocked up at Fran Moran's on the corner of Abbey Street, opposite Davy Tobin's the pawn office. This cinema also had a big balcony accessed by two wide concrete stairways on either side with marble effect finish. The doors to the main auditorium had those big posters for coming attractions in frames over each with stills on display in the outside windows.

At the Capitol you queued in the gutter of South Main Street with Mr Lacey shouting orders for to keep, 'Two deep now, two deep', to keep us from blocking the road. Tommy Swift sold his newspapers from a little pram-like contraption to the patrons of the evening shows. There was many a scuffle in that queue. Again going to the 'scratch' or 'four penny' hard wooden seats meant a different queue down in King Street. The Capitol had its own shop but much smaller than the

Abbey's. This shop probably did less business because there were a number of other options being on the Main Street. The more popular were O'Toole's and Murphy's (later Roche's) or O'Connor's little shop in the front room of a dwelling house in King Street. The Capitol had a very small balcony and it appeared to be reserved for priests and 'quality'. The Staffords often viewed the films from there. I think they owned the cinema. It was certainly housed in one of their many premises in that part of town in what used to be their furniture store. The next least expensive section of the Capitol was an area surrounded by wooden panelling. Even when prices were changing we called this 'the shillingy'. The next price down was six-pence before hitting the barrier for the 'scratch'. Another wonder of this cinema was the lady who walked around selling ice creams and ice-lollies from a tray. If you were in the money you might go for a tub of ice cream with the little wooden spoon and in later years there were bigger containers with red and green syrup stripes in it and with that you got a clear plastic spoon.

But The Cinema Palace was the place to be on a warm summer Saturday or a freezing rainy Winter Saturday. The first port of call on this route was Shudall's

Cinema Palace: Looking at this old poster we get an idea of how we came to call the Palace the Cinema Palace. The designer was using the rules of the day showing the name of the venue in the largest type and then fitting the other words in. Wexford people took the poster literally and read it from top to bottom. (Rossiter Collection)

shop at the corner of Gibson's Lane to stock up on the goodies as dispensed by the elderly Mrs Shudall (I assume) or her assistant Angie Molloy. This was a tiny little shop that could probably accommodate about four people at a time and I think they had a wooden form or bench at the wall opposite the counter. Thinking back it was probably a parlour of an old townhouse.

Then it was full speed ahead down Cinema Lane or officially but seldom used Harpur's Lane. If a stranger walked too quickly he would miss the cinema. There was no awning, no sign but we knew where it was. The building had been a warehouse before being converted into Wexford's first proper cinema back in 1914. In fact the first function held there was a concert in aid of Belgian refugees fleeing the Great War. In the cinema there was no separate shop. A young lady with bouffant hairstyle dispensed the tickets, the sweets, crisps and minerals, as soft drinks were called. Then you went up a few steps to be met by Mr Byrne who tore the ticket in half, impaled his portion on a needle and thread and kept an eye on you as you went to your seat. This observation was important because in this cinema there was no balcony and the division between the two prices of cushioned seats was noted only by different colour upholstery.

The abiding memory of the Cinema Palace is of Jeyes Fluid used to clean the premises. They even advertised the cinema at one time as being cleaned regularly with that substance. Sometimes if Mr Byrne was down the building looking after someone trying to upgrade himself or herself you dealt with Mrs Latimer at the door. She was the manageress.

We usually took our seats early and spent the intervening time chatting, eating and watching others arrive. The toilets in the Cinema were at the rear and had a sort of little hall leading to them. It was in this area that the projection booth was located and those in the know might have a chat with the projectionist who was known as 'Vistavision'.

There was no clock in the Cinema Palace. I don't think the Capitol had one either and that in the Abbey was not always right. We knew the pictures were about to start when Mr Byrne walked down the left aisle and started putting the wooden shutters on the windows. Then the lights dimmed and went out. On screen the advertisements started. There were hand made slides for local events like field days or local shops and forthcoming films. Then the first film started and a hush descended. Between films we had the national advertising and this was the time for using the toilets, restocking the food if there was money left or flinging weapons of not so mass destruction into the other sections of the cinema. All was quiet again for the main feature. They were usually westerns or 'cowboy pictures' in our day.

At the end of the film the lights came up, side doors opened and a wave of yelping young cowboys – and girls we presume but we seldom noticed them – flowed out into Cinema Lane. God help anyone unfamiliar with the town and its habits if they happened to be strolling up the lane. The film was revisited in a hundred young minds as we galloped on invisible horse and imitated 'the chap', as for some unknown reason we referred to the hero. Indians were massacred at the corner of South Main Street. Outlaws were hunted through the plains of Roche's Road and into Bride Street Churchyard. Going to the pictures may have had you sitting all afternoon but you got more than enough exercise heading home to the ranches of The Faythe, Bishopswater and Saint Aidan's. There were few obesity warnings then.

SATURDAY NIGHT

We were not yet old enough for discos, which were yet to be invented anyway, or dances so Saturday night was bath night. This usually meant an early call and a rather quiet night listening to the radio or later watching television.

Every few weeks it was haircutting time. For us that meant a visit from the barber on a bike, Jimmy Browne from Distillery Road. He arrived at a set time with his little brown suitcase filled with clippers, comb and scissors. He seems to have been a talented amateur because I believe he had a day job not at all connected to hair. He called to a number of houses in the street and with a bath towel hung round you, you got your hairstyle of the week, year or decade – a short back and sides, no variation on the theme. The man of the house usually had his done first, as he was probably off to the pub. They were not raving alcoholics. In fact most men only went to the pub on the Saturday night and maybe one other night. Remember money was short and hard work started early each morning so hangovers were not to be cultivated.

Domestic chores on the Saturday night usually included steeping the peas for the Sunday dinner, making jelly by dissolving the tablet of jelly in hot water and stirring until it was completely melted. Bacon was also steeped overnight.

Celebrating the Queen: It may not be too obvious but the badge on display on this highly fashionable coat depicts Queen Elizabeth and again shows the multi-cultural attitude of the 1950s. The location is just near The Bullring and the horse manure reminds us of the more common mode of transport of the period. (Rossiter Collection)

At Ferrybank

The old Thosel wall. Of note here especially is the pram with the deep base and big wheels in days before children travelled in fold-up buggies. Note also the 'Telefon' box.

Sunday stroll. This is South Main Street just beyond Coffey's Hill. The date is probably the 1950s judging by the fashions – hat, short trousers and the tansands being wheeled. The vehicular traffic consists of two cars and one ass and cart. The signs refer to R.Power, tryf accountant, and Wexford Brewery Stores.

O'Connor's Bakery Staff: Staff pictures were much more common back in the early 1900s. This group represent the workers of Frank O'Connor's Steam Bakery – motto, Bread is still the staff of life. (O'Connor Collection)

A former walled garden: This scene once backed onto the waterfront. The garden in question is to the rear of the building on North Main Street near Fettitt's Lane and the door visible through the gate would have been about 20 feet below street level, possibly leading into a cellar or basement. (Rossiter Collection)

Hill street in 1932: This is another picture of Wexford en-fete for the Eucharistic Congress. The view is up Hill Street.

Bannister Terrace: Today we call it Talbot Green. In my early years it was Talbot Street and earlier it was Bannister Terrace. This is another Eucharistic Congress scene.

SUNDAY MORNING

The primary objective of Sunday morning was Mass. In the days before the relaxation of the rules you had to be fasting from Midnight in order to receive Holy Communion.

This encouraged attendance at early Mass. Who wanted to starve until 11 o'clock or later? I usually attended 8.30 Mass with my father. It was in Rowe Street Church so he cycled with me on the crossbar. All that fasting gave you a fierce appetite so Sunday breakfast was special. There were usually rashers and sausages and that cholesterol missile, fried bread with lashing of brown sauce. We devoured that concoction with cups of strong hot tea.

After breakfast it was time to go to 'pay the society'. We usually combined this with a visit to my Aunt Kitty up in Batt Street. She lived in a wonderful little house that may well have been one of the first built in the street. There was a blacksmith's forge beside her and the road led past her house down to the Cott Safe and the sea. After a chat and meeting with the cousins we headed back down The Faythe to a little thatched house in among a row of other bigger houses. Even without the thatch you could not miss this place. Every Sunday morning there were queues of men outside.

The tontine society, to give it its proper name, was a bit like the club money. Ordinary people set it up and it was the ordinary working classes who joined. You got a special printed card with spaces for every week of the year. Each week the members paid a set amount in and this was collected in the tiny front room of that house – as were other societies in other parts of the town. If a member died, the society was notified – if they did not know already – and a 'death' was levied. This meant that every member had to pay a few pence extra and this was marked in another square. The family of the deceased then got a lump sum towards the funeral costs. This was the original basis of the society dating from the days of pauper burials. The weekly payments mounted and a few weeks before Christmas there were even bigger crowds queuing outside because they paid out the amount saved, less a sort of commission or administration fee. So you had a small-scale local financial institution offering a savings and life insurance scheme combined. Oh how boring it was going to pay the society. The adults loved it as a place get all the latest information or gossip and to discuss the forthcoming events from films to sport.

My father reared and kept canaries and other birds so the trip home diverted up Mulgannon to pick dandelions, which were a favoured delicacy for the birds. We would then cut down through Avenue de Flandres, probably annoying some of the residents who may have disliked the peasants using their little private road.

Sunday dinner was great but Sunday dessert was better although it usually consisted only of jelly and ice cream. The ice cream would have been bought as sixpenny wafers or a 'block' down in Goodison's shop in those days before home fridges.

Common Quay Street in the 1960s: Apart from the models of automobile on show the primary difference here is the old malt store on the site of the current Bank of Ireland building. The pub is The Slaney Bar and the cigarettes advertised are Gold Flake. Ita's offered wine and spirits while a sign between there and Wexford Motor Company advertised W Busher, car for hire, one of the old hackney drivers.

Wooden works at Clover: These were the remains, in the 1990s, of what appears to be an extension of the old Woodenworks extending out beside the Clover Meats Factory. (Rossiter Collection)

King Street 1932: The occasion is the Eucharistic Congress. Most towns in the country were decorated for the event. This is King Street with the Ropewalk Yard to the right with a huge tricolour flag. The houses in the left foreground were later demolished.

SUNDAY AFTERNOON

In those days Sunday was very much a family day but it was also a religious day and the afternoon combined both.

In our memories Sunday afternoons were always sunny and we were full of energy. The most common afternoon pursuit was visiting the dead either the recently deceased in Crosstown or the long dead at Carrig. Either trip seems daunting on foot now but we did them without a murmur. For Carrig it was a lovely pastoral stroll out Redmond Road where whole families went in convoy with those old high prams, tansads – the buggies of the era – and youngsters in Clarke's sandals. Do you remember them – brown, strapped and with white soles that had cleats in them?

At Carrig the families walked and prayed among the old gravestones, the children replayed the previous days film among the bushes and as the saying goes 'a marvellous day was had by all'.

The Crosstown trip was even more popular. Up until 1959 this took the walkers out Redmond Road and across the bridge at Carcur with its traffic calming measures using tar barrels and planks. Going out that way had its compensations in that we were often treated to a cornet – an ice cream cone - in Nolan's shop at The Monument. After 1959 the new bridge brought us to Crosstown but avoided that shop.

The walk over the bridge was brilliant in the sunshine. On the other side the youngsters walked along the low wall to Kaat's Strand and if permitted they went down on to the sand there to look at the old wreck of a boat that intrigued them. Then it was onward to the cemetery that has housed Wexford's dead since 1892. At the cemetery the graves of all deceased members of the family had to be visited. This could take some time with the wide-ranging families and friends but it was always accomplished and we still had the energy to traipse all the way home.

Sunday tea was always another special treat with sponge cake, tart or some other delicacy on offer to end a perfect and busy weekend.

III

Entertainment

RADIO

In today's world of every imaginable electronic device it is amusing to recall that half a century ago most of them were unheard of and even ones we knew about were exotic notions that were experienced only in other countries.

In the 1950s the main source of entertainment in the home was the radio or it was somewhat misleading called the wireless. It was far from wireless in that it was one of the few plug-in implements of the era. We had Irish dancing on radio with Dinjo. We followed the exploits of soap opera with *The Kennedys of Castleross* when they were the only Kennedys that mattered. We sang an Irish song with the *Walton's* programme and tuned in to fifteen minute 'sponsored' programmes to hear whatever music was popular at the time. On Sunday nights we had quizzes or *Question Time* broadcast from various locations around the country including the Abbey Cinema, Wexford. Hospitals Requests were broadcast on a Wednesday around lunchtime I think and we all listened, not because we had anyone in hospital but to hear the latest records. Not that there were many requests for people in Wexford County Hospital, as it was at the time. The most common name of hospital featured was Portiuncula and we all though that to be a very big establishment. The problems sorted out by 'Dear Frankie' must have either been censored or passed over our innocent heads just like *Come Fly With Me* sung by Frank Sinatra. Exotic names like Harry Thullier and Joe Linnane spewed from the big brown box in the corner with the light up dial. We knew nobody with names like that. This was all on Radio Eireann with its distinctive plonky version of *Roddy McCorley* as a signature tune.

On the long wave you tuned in to the BBC Light programme to listen avidly to *Children's Favourites* on a Saturday Morning presented by Bert Weedon. There we heard *Puff the Magic Dragon* or *The Old Woman Who Swallowed a Fly*.

My mother loved backing (betting on) horses so there was a regular ritual every weekday at four thirty. That was when the racing results were broad-cast on the BBC and if she was not home from town I took down the details. The winner had an X put by the name and second and third, or placed as that was called, got a tick. The winning odds were also noted. While wait-ing for the results we had to endure the boring British soap called *Mrs Dale's Diary*. I always imagined her as the sort of person living in Avenue de Flandres for some reason.

As time went by we were getting very sophisticated and scientific. From some-where, either on sale in kit form through comics or from a vendor in the Bullring, everyone was mad about crystal radio sets. It's a while since I saw one but as far as I can recall it was a plastic box affair with a few electrical items and a set of earphones. You set it up and carefully turned the dial to try to pick up a Medium Wave or what we now call AM station. More often than not you overshot the station and even when you did get it the sound was diabolical. But you listened avidly because this was cutting edge, this was your radio and it really was wireless, you had portable sound.

The next step forward was the transistor radio. These were a bit more expensive but they had real sound and easier tuning. In addition although you could use earphones, they were not essential. Adding to the power of the transistor was the arrival of real teenage music. First it was under the bedclothes Radio Luxembourg – earlier aficionados quote AFN or American Forces Network – and then pirate Radio Caroline. The young people of the 1960s probably spawned the ghetto blaster generation – on a smaller scale – because for years they seldom went any-where without musical accompaniment.

RECORD PLAYER

Believe it or not the world once existed without MP3, minidisks and CDs. In the 1960s the home entertainment 'must have', apart from the radio and television was the record player.

This had advanced considerably from the gramophone with the big horn and the old 78-rpm records when one song took up a twelve-inch disc. By the 1960s we had the six-inch single and the twelve-inch LP or long playing record. In between was the six-inch EP, which I think stood for equal play, whatever that meant, of four tracks.

All of these were played on the record player. The 'Dansette' was the most com-mon brand. Basically it was a square boxlike affair. The lid lifted to reveal a spindle and turntable and two dials or slotted controls. One of these controlled the speed or RPM (rotations per minute). For a single it was 45 rpm and an LP 33 rpm but

The Dansette record player that was the mainstay of teenage life in the early 1960s. (Rossiter Collection)

most of the record players included a 78-rpm setting. The other settings were for disc size at six or twelve inches. The volume and the more technical knobs of bass and treble were on the outer case beside the sound grille. The records, as we always referred to them never discs, could be stacked five deep on the spindle and would drop automatically as the previous one finished and the playing arm with its diamond stylus swung out of the way. As with all technology sometimes more than one record dropped down or the play arm went in too far a missed part of the song or most worrying the record fell on to the arm. At the cutting edge of technology, on some record players you could rotate the stylus for singles or LPs. The stylus had to be replaced regularly.

The humble record player was okay for the teenager but if adults wanted to play records they chose the radiogram. This was often a big mahogany or chestnut cabinet with the wireless and record player combined. It usually had presses on either side for the storage of records and the little velvety brush for cleaning the grooves. If the man of the house was handy he might knock up a cabinet to combine a wireless and record player in a sort of mock radiogram. There were lots of woodwork magazines with plans for these and a million other such projects on sale. The height of sophistication was to have a light bulb installed inside the record player section. My Granda had built one like that and I remember getting my first ever electric shock when I switched on that light with a wet hand. On the adult radiogram you were more likely to hear Jimmy Shand, John McCormack or the Gallowglass Ceili Band

As the listening public became more discerning the record players started to come with detachable stereo speakers and the LP covers sometimes had little boxes where you wrote the optimum settings for volume, bass and treble.

One of the few things I ever won was a truly portable record player. I think I won it in Dunne's Stores. It was a weird contraption where you could slot a six-inch record into it and actually carry it around as it played. The twin problems were - you needed a small truck to carry your stack of records as you strolled around and it scratched them as they were slotted in and out. Still, I suppose it foretold our modern permanent soundtrack to life players.

Dance Music: Long before pop charts and the like we had advertising for good music. Note the patriotic copy offering 'music of an Irish band recorded in the Free State'. The year was 1937. (Rossiter Collection)

COMICS AND READING

Our first comics were imported. No they weren't really imported. With almost every family having someone living and working in England or even America the parcel post did great business in the 1950s and early 1960s.

Aunts in England would send home clothes to the ladies of the family from the then exotic C&A stores and in most parcels would be a few sweets and one or two comics

The one I recall first is *Radio Fun*. It was black and white or if I am not mistaken a sort of black and pink. We didn't have a clue as to the characters but we devoured them and then swapped them through so many hands they became tattered. Swaps might be for 'lends' or 'for keeps'. Such was the barter system in full swing in that period. Pretty soon the English comics started to be sold locally. Was there a censorship going on initially or was it just that no one could afford them? We could then descend on Buckland's for our fix of reading material. For younger children there were *Jack and Jill* and *Playhour*. The slightly older had *The Dandy*, *The Beano*, *The Topper* or *The Beezer* every week.

The girls had *Bunty* and *Judy* among others. These were just the more popular of many titles. Parents must have seen a merit in the comics because most of us got a regular comic each Friday. With a bit of planning among our friends we managed to have a system whereby we got to read all the major titles. It was in these pages we met Biffo the Bear, Korky Kat, Dennis the Menace (the UK one with black spiky hair not the cute little American incarnation) and the main man Desperate Dan of the cow pie appetite.

Other comics that were popular at various stages in the period were *Buster*, *Victor* and *Roy of the Rovers*. As time went by more educational comics like *Look In* and Disney comics came on to the local shelves. Devouring every printed inch of these comics we first heard of Fleet Street and DC Thompson of Glasgow, wherever that was.

Somehow the indigenous industry never really competed in the comic's stakes. At school we did have *Our Boys* with the 'comic as Gaeilge' inside called *Tir Na nOg*. Even with an almost compulsory purchasing strategy especially in 'The Brothers' this combination never really dented our enthusiasm for foreign publications. The other, far from comic, publications offered to the youth of the day though the school were *The Far East* and *The Messenger* in its unique red cover.

At Christmas all the weekly comics published annuals. The big hard cover books with multiple stories featuring our entire favourite cast of characters plus puzzles and colouring pages. These were the bedrock of Christmas gift giving. Aunties vied with each other to get the most popular annual and of course the parent could not go wrong in having one or two under the tree.

Radio Fun

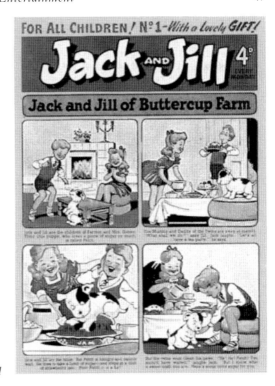

Jack and Jill

The *Beano*

The *Eagle*

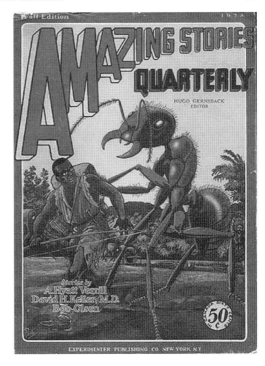

Amazing Quarterly

Classics Illustrated Huck Finn

On special occasions or when we had a few spare bob we invested in comics other than the weeklies. The most worthy of these were *Classics Illustrated*. These gave you exactly what they offered albeit with a classic story reduced to about 64 pages of full colour illustrations with speech bubbles. Whatever the limitation for purists, we got the gist of stories that might take weeks to read in a single sitting. All the classics were on offer from Dickens to HG Wells and we devoured them.

Then we moved on to contemporary works like Batman and Superman and the super heroes of the American continent. These were provided through Marvel, Dell and DC Comics. There were a few types on offer. The most popular were the full colour publications of the more popular heroes. There was also some veering into the horror genre with lurid and often grisly covers. In general these were in black and white only inside. A major feature of these American publications was the advertising. It was here that we first met Charles Atlas and were promised bodies of steel. We could also buy x-ray glasses or telescopes that revealed all or we could buy eggs that developed in days into weird creatures. Naturally with prices in dollars and delivery times in months we never speculated our hard earned cash on these. The British comics were different in their items advertised and in the fact that some of us did purchase, sending postal orders to odd addresses like PO Box 911, Hemel Hampstead. The big seller in these UK comics was stamps. We were all going to be millionaires from philately. They offered bags of stamps for a few shillings with a free album and a bonus free magnifying glass to spot those important features of the stamps. They were usually advertised with a 'penny black' and I suppose we all expected to get a major find that Stanley Gibbons had missed. The stamps were stuck into the albums with weird little adhesive rectangles.

One thing I do remember buying from an advert in a comic was a 'five in one' gadget. It turned out to be a plastic gizmo that offered binoculars, compass, mirror, microscope and magnifying glass.

Back to the comics and we progressed yet again as we got older to a sub genre that many adults also read. If you see the words 'Achtung' and 'Banzai' and you are of the right age you will recognise these. They were called 'sixty four pages' because that was the page count and the pages measured about five inches by four inches. The subject matter was mostly westerns or war and they were published monthly in sets of titles.

From there or perhaps earlier in some cases we moved on to books like *The Famous Five*, *Nancy Drew* or *Biggles*. Getting older still we resorted to two magazines that in retrospect were probably more like teenage comics. These were *Weekend* and the double entendre sounding *Titbits*. These were slightly sensationalist – for the time – with slightly revealing pictures, human interest and show business tales and nuggets of useless trivia. From there people began to specialise depending on their hobbies or interests. *Photoplay* was a very popular publication for the film buff while every pop group seemed to have a monthly fan magazine.

War Library – Banzai

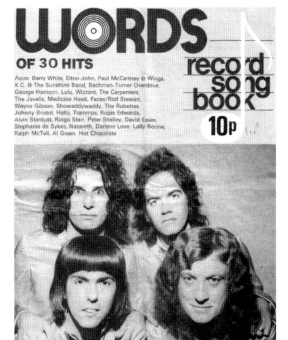

Words: This was the magazine
with the song words that was
swapped and re-swapped.
(Foley Collection)

For the general pop fan it was hard to beat a monthly that offered the lyrics of all the hits of the charts. It was called *Words – record songbook*. It was bought, studied and swapped but God knows if anyone sang the words. Swapping was the order of the day and it meant that from our *Playhour* days up to *Photoplay* we got to read dozens of publications every month.

We were oh so cosmopolitan in those days.

TELEVISION

Television was the main influence on our generation. We were just old enough when Radio Telefis Eireann opened on New Years Eve 1961 to be awestruck by this new medium.

Television rental shops had sprung up all over Ireland in the run up to the opening. I don't know what people away from the east coast watched on those televisions bought before the initial broadcast. Here we could splash out on extra aerials for BBC and HTV (the Welsh version of ITV). We didn't go the 'whole hog' we only got the long narrow aerial for HTV and didn't bother with the 'H' shaped BBC one. It was a source of snobbery to look at chimneys in those days to see who was posh enough to have a television and then how many aerials they had. Regardless of the number of aerials most people still paid 'the few bob a week' to the rental company.

The initial television sets were commonly the 17-inch variety. They were far from reliable and the engineers from RTV and such companies were in great demand for re-tuning and general repairs. The sets had twiddly little buttons at the back to adjust 'horizontal hold' and 'vertical hold'. The younger people became expert tuners using these as they stretched round the behemoth sets. A miniscule turn too much and the picture went 'rolling' or else seemingly fell over on its side to give a lined pattern. Then all hell broke loose as everyone thought they were THE expert at adjust the problem. When that was fixed there was brightness and contrast to adjust. Sometimes the reception was so bad that you might as well have been watching the programme through a snowstorm but still we watched. One 'expert' remedy for bad reception was to put a bit of paper around the aerial connection in the back of the set. It sometimes worked because the problem had resulted from the connection getting loose. This happened because initially you had to plug in the different aerial wire to change programmes. The first innovation to remedy this was to have the cables – which entered through a hole bored in the window frame – end in connection boxes screwed to the window sill.

Tops of the Town: This was one of the entertainment hits of the 1960s and 1970s playing to full houses and showcasing the great talent hidden in our shops and factories. This group is representing Woolworth's. Participants are Celine Busher, Mary Butler, Maura O'Connor, Nancy Goodison, Teresa Roche, Anne Doyle, Madeleine Doran, Margie Coughlan, Betty Leacy, Margaret Carroll, Maria Hayes, Kay Butler, Kathleen Saunders, Mary O'Connor and Mary Moynihan. (O'Leary Collection)

Outing: Pub and factory outings were a great feature of life in Wexford in the late 1900s. These might be day trips to a beauty spot or to a sporting event. Money was collected weekly to pay for the bus, the meal and, of course, the drink that was carried in wooden crates in the luggage compartment. (Rossiter Collection)

Rehearsal: Wexford has been a musical and entertainment centre for centuries with
bands, opera, Tops and others. This picture is probably from the 1960s and shows
rehearsals for The Mikado. The players include Kevin O'Mahoney, Oliver Sinnott, Sean
Meyler, Des Corish and another who I cannot identify. (Rossiter Collection)

FESTIVAL FORUM

SATURDAY, OCTOBER 31st AT 8.30 P.M.

MRS. ARTHUR LANIGAN-O'KEEFFE
RT. HON. VICOUNT BOYD OF MERTON, C.H., ex-Cabinet Minister
MR. BILL THOMSON, Canadian Painter and Musician
MR. HUW WHELDON, B.B.C. TV. personality
Chairman: MR. FINTAN M. O'CONNOR, L.L.B.

Open to the public, who are invited to send in questions.

Booking at Wexford 50.
10 a.m. to 12 noon; 2.30 p.m. to 4.30 p.m.; 7 p.m. to 10 p.m.
ADMISSION 7/6 and 5/-

Festival Forum: This gives an indication of the speakers gracing the stage at the forum.
(Rossiter Collection)

The Third
WEXFORD
FESTIVAL

PERAQUAM ET IGNEM

Music and the Arts

October 25 – November 1

1953

Wexford Festival 1953: This is the front of the programme for the festival in that year. (Rossiter Collection)

To protect our eyes from the glare shops started selling rolls of blue tinted cellophane. This was draped over the screen and held in place by an ornament on the top of the set. After 1963 plastic busts of John F Kennedy and Pope John the Twenty-third performed this task admirably. Those were the old black and white days so some bright spark convinced people that looking at the television through coloured sweet wrappers made it look like being in colour.

In those early years we would watch almost anything on television. We had favourites like *Have Gun Will Travel, The Virginian, The Thin Man* and *Francis Durbridge Theatre*. Some home produced programmes had special connections. *The School Around the Corner* was a 'must see' because our cousin Paddy Crosbie was the presenter and Thelma Ramsay who played the accordion was married to another cousin, Martin Crosbie. A decade later in 1971 we were watching *The Partridge Family, Mary Tyler Moore* and *The Riordans*. So it went until we entered the multi-channel and satellite ages.

TOYS

Without a doubt the most important toy for boys in those days was the gun. These ranged from silver-plated six shooters through derringers and rifles to German lugers.

The rifle that I remember best was about three feet long with a white plastic stock, a black barrel and a silver inset where the roll of caps was inserted. Like most exotic weapons this was a Christmas present – in that season of peace and goodwill to all mankind.

Another weapon that I can visualise still was the German luger pistol with the black metal and the brown grip. We didn't make any value judgements on the original wielders of such guns. To us they were fun toys and looked and felt great.

Most of us would have started off with the little tin cap gun. These weighed little or nothing and probably cost a few pennies. They often appeared in Christmas stockings. More often than not they were so out of line that they failed to hit the little bubble in the roll of caps and so were useless. Quite often if we got fed up with this useless gun we took out the roll of caps, placed it on a rock and bashed it with another rock (or hammer if one was available) to produce a tremendous bang. Who recalls buying those rolls of caps in little paper cylinders down in George Bridge's?

In later years fancier replicas became available. These looked just like the snub nosed guns the private eye used in the films or the little derringer favoured by the gamblers in the old West. These usually took a different type of explosive force in the shape of a single tab of powder encased in paper. They usually made even louder noise.

Matchbox truck

Cork guns were popular for younger children. These worked on some sort of pneumatic principle. They were 'cocked' by bending. This pulled back a lever and a mechanism in the barrel. The cork came attached to a piece of string secured to the gun. When you pulled the trigger it shot out all of two feet until the string activated. That was not very exciting so we usually severed the string or else used these guns to shot pebbles, bits of cardboard or some other missiles that mothers always warned would 'cut the eye out of someone'.

Another gun that was common was the spud gun. This also gave us the rudiments of physics and pneumatic pressure. It was 'cocked' and the nozzle plunged into a raw potato. A piece of the potato wedged in the barrel and on firing it flew towards the target, person or thing we aimed at.

I remember the excitement in the early 1960s when one member of our group got a 'real' cowboy holster in brown leather from an aunt or cousin who worked in America. For some reason it was a left hand holster only but even the least ambidextrous of us vied for 'a lend' if this fantastic item.

Of course the guns were augmented by other items like rubber daggers, cowboy suits of 'chaps' and a waist coat with frills or tassels – how many pioneers wore such garb in Montana? There was also the sheriff's badge or even the marshal's badge – even at 7 or 8 years of age we knew the difference. We also had the hats with a long string so that we didn't lose them as we galloped on invisible horses across a Wexford prairie. Somehow Indian gear, headdresses, rubber tomahawks and bows and arrows did not have the same appeal although we did have them. Maybe it was because in such a get up you were predestined to die in the early part of the game.

Not that all toys were bloodthirsty. Dinky cars were a perennial favourite. These exact replicas of cars that seldom if ever graced a Wexford road were admired, coveted and saved for. The primary outlets were George Bridge's in Selskar or O'Toole's in South Main Street. The cars came individually packed in cardboard boxes and many a Saturday morning would be spent looking and occasionally buying in one of those shops of delight. Later came the Matchbox cars. These were, as the name suggests, small versions of the same cars – about a third the size of a Dinky. They were cheaper and therefore more accessible so many youngsters started collecting these. My father made a garage for my collection with a ramp from the roof and a little lift or elevator operated by twine.

As we got older we graduated to Scalextric or some cheaper version thereof. This was the height of fashion with cars whizzing around an electric track controlled by a little plastic device with a plunger, held by the participants. That was the plan but we spent more time putting the cars back on the track after spinning or shooting off than we did racing.

Most youngsters also went for trains and tracks. These ranged from clockwork to electric and some enthusiasts even bought little model people, animals and buildings to go with them. For me putting the slot together tracks into figure-of-eight and setting the clockwork engine pulling two carriages and a coal tender was about enough. That is unless you count having a few model soldiers mown down by the train as they foolishly stood on the tracks. The enthusiasts bought Hornby train sets while we usually went for the cheaper Triang. Meccano was the toy for budding engineers who constructed all types of cranes and cars and marvellous objects. It was the Lego of that generation.

Collecting model soldiers was another youthful obsession. Early on these were deadly – in every sense of the word – lead soldiers from knights to World War Two snipers that we sometimes painted ourselves. Mass production plastic brought the prices down and the variety of figures up. Now we had colourful cowboys and Indians, horses, covered wagons, stagecoaches and buffaloes to inhabit our make believe world. How many of these ended up mangled by lawnmowers is a mystery because we positioned so many in a lawn that became the Great Plains we always forgot to collect them all.

Later came really miniature soldiers. These came in boxes of about a hundred. They were unpainted and had men about a half inch high. You got quantity but the drab single colour throughout was not conducive to great playtime quality. Airfix models of planes and tanks were also popular but to be honest unless you had some artistic talent they ended up a mess of plastic, glue and smeared paint in the end.

For more sedate periods we resorted to board games. At the time the choice was much more limited that today. You usually had Ludo, Snakes & Ladders or Draughts. Chess was for the swots.

IV

The Seaside

Wexford is a seaside town but it is, or was, a working port so the residents wanting a beach usually had to travel a distance.

But there were a few options within walking distance. The ones that spring to mind include Ferrybank and Kaat's Strand.

Ferrybank is on the eastern end of the current bridge and since 1959 has been almost on our doorstep. Prior to that it required a trek out Redmond Road, across the old bridge and back towards town. The beach, if we could call it that, was not the best. In the main it consisted of a small strip of rough sand on the shore facing the town. It was fine for a paddle. At the time there was not a lot of reclaimed land to your back as you looked across to the quay. The area of the road down to the trawlers and the land in between is a result of dumping dredged material from the harbour works there. In earlier times the tides from the seaward side washed in almost to the concrete leading from the bridge toward the breakwater. So we had sand on either side. The Ardcavan side was a great source of fishing bait and cockle picking at that time and hordes of people could be seen out there at low tide with sprongs and sacks in hand.

Ferrybank in the days before the opening of the swimming pool was the venue each year for swimming and water safety lessons. Working purely from a memory I think a Guard Greene was involved in that at the start. Lessons took place from a little wooden jetty.

Today we have trawlers moored out at Ferrybank but a few decades ago the main attraction out there was the strand and a walk along the concrete area towards the breakwater. That breakwater – the line of rocks stretching out to The Black Man – was constructed in the early 1800s. It must have been a massive undertaking using horses and carts and manual labour. It does what the title suggests, breaks the waves coming into the harbour before they can cause any damage, and so gives a calm working harbour.

The other beach near town on this side is the wonderfully named Kaat's Strand on the way out to Crosstown. In many ways this is probably a misnomer. It is not a fancy spelling for Cat's as some people – usually blow-ins – may think. It

Picnic on Browne's Bank: For many especially in the south end of town this was the trip to the seaside. Browne's Bank was just over the railway lines below Batt Street. (Rossiter Collection)

refers to a Mr Van Kaat who had a shipyard at Westgate back in the 1600s. Why he would have had a strand across a river that was not traversed by a bridge at the time is a mystery. One possibility is that the original Kaat's Strand was at Westgate Lane before the reclamation work undertaken by Redmonds left it landlocked.

In the 1960s there was an old wreck stranded here and it was a great attraction for youngsters as families headed out to visit the cemetery. The strand was fairly wide at low tide and had better sand than Ferrybank. It was and still is a popular fishing area.

At the south end of town there was less in the way of sandy beaches. Heading out from the Trinity Street area you could access some nice stony seaside areas. Maybe the people from that part of town, more traditionally associated with seafaring, were less interested in going to the seaside after spending a working life on the sea. One place I remember is 'Browne's Bank'.

It was an area with lovely springy grass where adults could picnic while the children played in the water within easy reach and sight. Going down Batt Street accessed the bank. At the end of that street you went down a hill bordered by wooded rails that may have been constructed from old railway sleepers. The view from there was stunning on a sunny day in decades sadly gone. On the left jutting out into the water was a reclaimed area with Clover Meats factory and The Star Iron Works. In front was the cott safe, an enclosed manmade harbour dotted with boats of all the most vivid colours on blue water with others pulled up on the shingle strand. These were the personal craft of people living in the town but were not the dinghies and yachts we now associate with landlubbers. These were working boats that might be sailed everyday or just after work in the factories to fish or to transport goods. They might also be sports craft waiting for one of the many regattas that took place throughout the county at the time to be sailed or rowed in competition. Another common use of these boats was to travel to Rosslare Strand, especially the burrow area.

Rosslare Strand, and we must make the distinction of strand rather than harbour because they were very much separate entities, was the primary seaside destination of Wexford people. This is because from the earliest days of rail travel it was on the route and there were regular scheduled services. Remember cars were few and far between before the 1970s. Rosslare Strand attracted two distinct visitors. There were day-trippers and summer residents.

For a day trip Sunday was the most popular day and CIE cashed in on the mania by putting on lots of trains. These operated from two stations – yes Wexford was big enough to have two – the present North Station (officially O'Hanrahan Station) and the South Station, just past The Talbot Hotel. Being from the south end of town we usually used the South Station but for the thrill of travelling along the quayside on the Woodenworks – actually you travelled beside it – sometimes we walked up to the other station.

Late Sunday mornings in a sunny summer could be like scenes from films set in India. After attending Mass families loaded up their bags. Into these went primus stove, kettle, cups, sandwiches, cutlery, biscuits and myriad necessities. These were real cups and things, paper and plastic were some years off. You can imagine the weight of the bags. The children were also packing up. For them it was tin buckets and spades along with the towels and togs and the big tartan rug so often used for picnics.

The South Station was actually more impressive than the North. Here the Rosslare bound train arrived on the seaward platform and the 'up train' went to the landside. Hundreds of people crowded on to the platform each fine Sunday. There were tee shits, khaki short pants, flowery dresses, straw hats, flat caps, cardigans, pullovers and plastic macs to beat the band. Youngsters amused themselves 'pegging' stones into the water of the harbour just feet away. Daredevils crossed the tracks and sat on the harbour wall. The ladies crowded into the little waiting room with its bench, ticket office and pot-bellied stove. Heads craned out over the platform edge. In the days of steam they watched for the plume of smoke as the train approached the quay. The smart-arses watched the signals and competed to be first to say, 'She's on the way'.

Then the big black engine rounded the bend. People shuffled and vied for a good position to rush aboard. Mothers grabbed at children too close to the edge. 'Come're ye'll be kilt' was a common cry.

Through the years the carriages changed. In the early days there were three classes from First to Third. The carriages originally were without connection. You got in the door and had cushioned seats on either side of you and that was it. Later there were carriages that you entered at either end. You went up the corridor and chose a compartment that seated about eight people and was entered through a sliding glass door. It was only in more recent times you got the present configuration.

The corridor trains were very popular for a number of reasons. You could see who was in the compartment before you entered and could decide if you wanted to sit with them.

Another advantage was that children could stay in the corridor. This was great for looking out the window as the train chugged down what we would now advertise as a wild coastline. Heads were stuck out from the windows at the doors. Remember the windows let down on a leather strap? Faces were smeared with smuts and debris but it was an adventure. You had to be careful at that because the conductor or ticket collector would give out yards to you for sticking your head out. In those days he might give you a clip in the ear too.

At Rosslare Strand the passengers poured out and down Station Road. The bulk of them turned left at the end round the post office and shop of Lamberts, unless they were visiting locals or summer residents. There was a café with a lovely green area beside it at this junction.

Every family had its own destination at the strand – we never called it a beach – these probably became popular through generations. There were lanes, roads or maybe just little trails leading through the dunes to access these locations. Going down on to the sand was not very popular. Families usually set up camp on the grassy areas among the sheltering hills. The rug was placed and the bags deposited. The mammy set about unpacking and the children raced off to the sand and sea with the daddy, often in his suit or on really hot days stripped down to trousers, pullover and flat cap, keeping an eye on the kids from the edge of the dunes.

At Rosslare the strand was already sporting conservation works in the 1960s. There were wooden fences stretching from dunes out into the sea. These were great for youngsters jumping over as they raced along. They also provided dare-devil walkways out into the water with waves washing over feet. In addition they were impromptu diving boards once the togs were on. As people tired these also served as places to dig out crabs while younger children made sand castles on the shore.

When hunger took hold people returned to the dunes where the mammy had been busy boiling the kettle on the primus stove after getting it filled by a friendly resident. Some people dispensed with the primus and bought a kettle of boiled water from the café. I suppose the more well off people in sitting in for their tea and cakes looked down their noses on them.

With the tea made there was the usual battle of getting children to eat a sandwich – usually banana or cheese – before starting on the biscuits. If you had a few bob you might go for an ice cream or even a choc-ice after the food. Then you had to wait an hour before being allowed back into the water.

The days went all too quickly and soon the adults were looking at the watch. It

Rosslare Strand: The high building on the left was the Coastguard Station – later converted to holiday apartments. The buildings in the dunes are NOT the huts referred to in the article, these are much more substantial edifices but they were gone in the early 1960s. (Lawrence Collection)

Rosslare Harbour: this is a fine view of Rosslare Harbour on a sunny day as passengers prepare to board the train. (Lawrence Collection)

was time to pack up and head for the station.

Everyone headed back to the station early. There must have been a phobia about being late and missing the train. This did not bother the children too much because the station area at Rosslare was a natural playground. There were grassy banks around the station and a ramp and platform – like the ones that used to be outside farms to load milk churns onto carts – that drew children like magnets. The main attraction of this station was the huge – well huge to youngsters – grass covered bank that led down from the road bridge. This was ideal for sliding down on a lump of cardboard and to add to the joy, there were steps to climb back up. The bank looked like a war zone every Sunday evening as the train pulled away. The long grass was battered flat and shiny and hundreds of pieces of brown cardboard boxes were strewn around. I wonder where the cardboard came from?

Back in Wexford the hordes disembarked and trudged wearily but happily home exhausted and bright red from the sunburn.

Rosslare also attracted families who stayed at the strand for weeks or even months. The majority of these stayed in huts they owned or rented on a weekly basis. The huts ranged from the basic one room with outside chemical toilet to your little mini home. Caravans and eventually mobile homes followed before giving way to summer homes.

I remember staying in two such huts as a guest of the family of one of my friends. The first one was a red pained hut up on the banks below the coastguard station. I would estimate that it measured about fifteen feet by fifteen. It was of timber construction with either a felt or galvanised roof and two windows. The toilet was a sort of sentry box with a bucket under a seat. It slept four as I recall, on beds that swung down from the walls and fold up canvas beds not unlike old stretchers on legs. In later years the family moved to a slightly larger hut in a field beside a farmyard. The field had about a dozen other structures from huts to mobile homes.

Transporting the family to Rosslare for this holiday was no mean feat. If the family or a friend did not have a car they had to hire a hackney car. These were the only cars most people saw the insides of in those days and then it was usually only for weddings or funerals. Three that I recall offering the service were Syl Carley, Chris Hopkins and Kevin Kehoe. There were probably others and definitely the undertakers like Con Macken and Willie Parle offered the service. How a family loaded the week's provisions, clothes and other necessities plus the children into those Austin Cambridges and other such models is a mystery.

Staying at the seaside for a prolonged period was an adventure. You could be at the beach first thing in the morning or as the moon shone. You had a big field with briars and furze bushes to play in with newfound friends. The farmyard gave you an insight into rural living without you even realising it. One thing I do recall was walking barefoot to the strand from the hut through the farmyard trying to avoid both stones and cow pats – we didn't bring shoes down because someone would have to look after them

Another major attraction if you stayed in Rosslare Strand was the possibility of attending a real dance in a real hotel. The Golf Hotel held children's dances every Thursday from 7.00 until 9.00 p.m. Well they were real to us even if it was only music from a record player and a bottle of minerals. Not that there was much interactive or inter-gender dancing at the session, but it was oh so sophisticated to us.

Another seaside occupation was caddying at the golf club or golf links as the Rosslare club was designated. Not many of us got to do this but I hear there was good pocket money to be had. What we did get to do on the golf links was to look for lost golf balls and sell them back to the members. I never made a penny at that either.

The wreck: This was a magnet for young people on the beach at Rosslare Strand. It was an old coaster long run aground and filling up with sand. It was a sad rusting wreck but to us it could be anything from a pirate ship to an aircraft carrier where we could re-live last week's trip to the 'pictures'. (Rossiter Collection)

By the seaside in the 1950s. Note the pre-plastic era tin bucket and spade. (Rossiter Collection)

Today people have time-shares and holiday villas in Malaga or Lanzarote but all that probably grew from those huts in Rosslare.

To the north of Wexford Curracloe was growing in popularity but really you needed a car for a family visit or to stay because there was no train. Some people did have huts and later caravans but essentially it was a day trip option. My visits there in the early days were restricted to when Madge and Pat or Lil and Ginger came home from England on their annual holidays. Sometimes they hired a hackney car to go out there and in latter years they or their friends the O'Briens or their pal Jackie Jackson had a hire car. Apart from the wide expanse of beach the main attraction was The Winning Post opened in 1946. This has now grown to an amusement centre from its origins as a little sweet and ice cream shop.

As we grew older we often cycled out to Curracloe. After that long ride it was great to reach the Strand Hotel, look down at the Winning Post and the rushes on either side of the road and either free wheel or race down the hill. I wonder is that why they called it the Winning Post? Facing the hill at the start of the journey home, tired, sunburnt and sandy it didn't seem half as attractive.

As we became more affluent and cars became more common we spread our wings and explored Blackwater with its little whitewashed cottage by the river, Ballyhealy and Cullenstown or Ballytrent and other places that were basically sea and sand.

Kilmore Quay offered a wild and windswept rough beach as well as the pier to explore and the boats to admire. Carne had similar attractions but on a smaller scale with the wild Atlantic beach at Carnsore close by to marvel at huge waves. Duncannon was probably the furthest we ventured and even then it was usually to stay with Saint Joseph's Club in the fort for the annual holiday.

Looking back to the seaside all we see is sunshine, blue sky and blue water but surely it rained sometime.

V

Sweets

Think childhood and you have to think sweets.

They were the currency of life. They were the reward for favours done or being 'good'. They were the sanction imposed if behaviour left something to be desired. They were the 'protection money' paid to the bully and the sharing 'wampum' of good friends.

Some of the old sweets are still with us like Bounty although this is no longer advertised with people seeking satisfaction on desert islands as bounty hunters. Others are still available but under new names so let's concentrate on the oldies that the new generation cannot buy.

The Flash bar was a great treat. This bar of hard toffee covered in chocolate was a great treat especially when by some manufacturing quirk the chocolate was thicker than usual. For a cheap chocolate bar there was the Macaroon bar. This was inferior quality chocolate with coconut flavour pieces.

In Ally Whites you could buy Spearmint bars. These came without any printing on the wrapper other than a sort of cobweb design. Who recalls 'Fry's Five Centres' sometimes called Fry's Assortment? It was an ingenious concoction with five different flavours as you ate through it. The other biggie from Fry's was the Chocolate Cream with its white minty centre in dark chocolate. Oh and not to forget those belly dancing ladies advertising the other Fry's treat – Turkish Delight.

Opal Fruits made our mouths water as the advertisement programmed us. Spangles were a poor relation either in mint or fruit flavours. They were rock hard as opposed to the chewy Opals. In the world of chewy but gorgeous Cadburys had most of the trump cards.

Aztec brought us into ancient lands with fudge covered chocolate with peanuts. Some saw it as a poor relation of the Mars Bar. Marathon was similar but with the nuts inside. Meanwhile Picnic gave you the same ingredients but in a more irregular bundle. These later became Lion Bars. Curley Wurley was just weird. It was a toffee bar covered in chocolate with irregular holes in it. Milky Way was the 'probiotic' marketing of the era. This was the 'sweet you can eat between meals without ruining your appetite'. It probably worked because there was little in it.

Éclairs turned the world on its head. Here you got round pieces of toffee with a bit of chocolate in the centre. Toffos were similar but without the chocolate. Back then we would eat anything. Never let the foodies tell you that colour matters. We ate Wham bars that could only be described as pink with yellow or green fizzy bits.

For strong teeth and long lasting enjoyment there was little to beat the black and white striped Bull's-eye or its close but much hotter cousin the Clove Ball in red and white. The latter also came in rock form. A smaller suckable was the little brown Aniseed Ball with the miniscule liquorice tasting centre.

Love hearts had little in the way of taste – a bit perfumy – but there was eating and reading in them. Refreshers were tingly especially the earlier variety with the smooth concave side. Another fizzy was Sherbet, but we always called it Sherbert, in its many guises. It came in a rolled package with a bit of liquorice as a straw to suck it out and was called a fountain. It also came in bags with a little lollipop to suck and dip back in wet to let the powder stick to it. Space Dust was the dangerous mutation of Sherbet. There were addiction and damage potential scares about this with tales of it exploding in the mouth. I never witnessed that but too much could explode out your nose with very unedifying consequences.

For the hot sunny summers we switched to the fridge. There we had Sparklers, single flavour ice pops, Rockets, a different flavour on the fuselage and pod with sometimes a thin chocolate coating on the tip, Orange Split, ice pop exterior and ice cream inside on to the top choice of the Choc Ice. That was the pre-Magnum era.

Down the scale came Dolly Mixtures in horrid little plastic bags. These were real 'kiddies' sweets.

The more sophisticated 'smoked' sweet cigarettes complete with red tip. They might also eat Pez in the wild and wonderful dispensers that cost more than the little tiny packs of sweets. No matter what age we were we loved the Selection Box that cornerstone of Christmas with the variety of bars and bags with the added extra of a game or a picture to colour. Remember the games always need that cut out piece with a matchstick through it to use instead of dice?

Chewing Gum and Bubblegum were also popular but these had to add the collector's cards of film stars or sporting heroes to boost sales. Another item that contained sweets but was not strictly speaking for this section was the Lucky Bag. This surprise bag of rubbish must have kept thousands of sweated labour industries going for years. Feel them as much as you could before buying you still got trash. It was either a whistle or a yoyo or some other useless and soon broken toy. You also scored a small bar or two tiny toffee sweets. The gene that spawned the Lotto was already in place because you kept buying hoping for that secret slip offering you the mystery prize – one per box of 144 Lucky Bags – that was equally useless but we had the bug.

MORE and BETTER
by the World's Largest Manufacturers
of Pure Sugar Hard Candies.

CHARMS Co. • Bloomfield & Asbury Park, N. J.

Cherry
Orange
Lemon
Lime
Crystal Mint
Wintermint
Peppermint
Grape
Peach
Butterscotch
Rum & Butter
Coffee
Pineapple
Raspberry
Assorted
And All-Spice

Charms

Lucky Numbers

Into the courting days of course you had to graduate in your choice of sweets. Milk Tray was around and of course none of us knew the 'secret of the Black Magic Box'. Roses 'grew on you' with a comedian Norman Vaughan making a packet in the adverts. Lucky Numbers had you choosing the centres by number while Double Centres gave twice the enjoyment.

I'm sure I missed a favourite of yours but maybe all that sugar has affected my memory. The only thing you will probably say is that they tasted better back then but then again maybe that's rose tinted taste buds or the fact that we did not have the chance to over indulge at the time.

VI

Looking Back

THE YEAR 1954

This was the Marian Year and there were shrines and prayer meeting throughout the country.

A major event of the year was at Our Lady's Island where Father Peyton known as the 'rosary priest' was to preach. This was part of his international crusade. As a result of the crowds expected even in those days of not so many family cars, traffic plans were put in place. There would be one-way traffic systems in the area with access to the island via Killinick, Broadway and St. Ivers while those leaving would go through Tagoat and Killinick. A fleet of 32 buses would leave pilgrims off and collect them at St. Ivers.

There was tragedy in August of that year when two young men were drowned in Wexford Harbour. They were first cousins and had got into difficulty near the pump station on the North Slob. Sadly, one of the bodies was not found until later in the year when it appeared on the Welsh coast. The tragedy reminded people of the infamous drownings going to Ardcavan Races just over a half century earlier.

Pasteurised milk arrived in Wexford that year too. It was in August 1954 that what was to become Snowcream bought the old Mercy School in George Street from JJ Stafford to build the facility to pasteurise milk and sell it at six old pennies a pint. That was in glass bottles – remember them? They had to be washed and left out on the windowsill each night, often with a note stuck in the neck of the bottle to the milkman requesting an extra pint.

The year was bad for rabbits in County Wexford with the arrival of myxomatosis that disfigured and killed thousands of the creatures and turned many off rabbit stew for life.

Mercy School: This is a group photograph of teachers and pupils of the Mercy School that was located in Upper George's Street. It was later the site for Snowcream. The picture probably dates from the early 1900s. (O'Connor Collection)

THAT OLD-TIME RELIGION

Not more than a few years ago there were the days of gender segregation at least regarding religion.

You could not have men and women praying in the same seats at the same time. Men and women sat at different sides in the churches – much like bride and groom families at weddings. The segregation used to extend to confession boxes with men on one side and women on the other. I bet those were uneven queues. Remember also that women had to have hats, scarves or veils in those days and churching was an important ceremony after childbirth.

Who remembers swapping tales about easy and hard confessors or stories of priests shouting at people in confession? Then there was the decision on which queue was moving quicker. That was very important with confession to be attended every Saturday morning as well as going down town on messages and getting back in time to go to the matinee cinema in the afternoon.

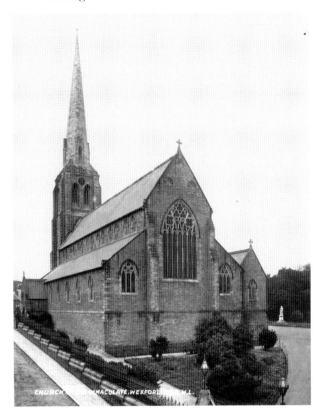

Rowe Street Church:
This is a nice pastoral
view of the church.
(Lawrence Collection)

The confraternity was the bane of our lives. I cannot recall whether it was on a Wednesday or a Thursday evening but my memory does know that it was always the sunniest evening of the week. To add to the torment, the Boy's Confraternity was held in Rowe Street, miles away and having it at 5.30 in the evening ripped the day apart.

Not that we ever missed attending. No we were not sacred – we were scared. Every section in the confraternity had a prefect and every prefect had a book. These books had the names and if you failed to turn up there were questions asked in class the following day – by the Brothers.

As I recall the confraternity evening was divided between rosary, sermon and benediction with its Latin hymns like *Tantum Ergo*. The church was divided into sections with shield like standards marking the set of seats designated for each. My abiding memory of the events are the smell of incense and the hymn *Faith of Our Fathers* which was a rousing piece but also a signal that the prayers were over for another week. It was always the final hymn. That particular hymn was also linked to the annual parish retreat and the less frequent mission that occurred around every five years.

I never recall missions like those featured in the writings of John B. Keane and Patrick Kavanagh but there was a certain atmosphere about the town when the mission was on. The missioners – always drafted in from outside – were a topic of discussion. Which was the hardest, which was easiest for confession. They were sighted as they traversed the streets making house calls. Did you want to be in or out when they called? They seemed to manage to get to every house at some time in their three-week stay. They were here for three weeks – a week each for children, women and men, usually in that order. The missions were so popular that children were sent in early to keep seats for the Ma.

In the week of the men's retreat shares in Brylcreem and soap must have rocketed. The whiff of soap and hair oil was overpowering and the shining skin dazzling.

It is a sign of the power of religion in those times that the cinemas did not open until after the ceremonies during the mission. Hell fire and damnation were the reported themes of the adult missions. Thinking back I wonder if they were wasting their time on the converted or whether the shouting and roaring are what had them converted.

Another religious feature of the Wexford and Irish home was the Sacred Heart lamp. This highly specialised bulb with a crucifix shaped element was almost compulsory in a Catholic home. It burned 24 hours a day, seven days a week in front of the picture of the Sacred Heart. The priest usually signed the picture after he had blessed the home when the family moved in. Most Wexford people bought such pictures from the Adoration nuns or in Matty Furlongs shop. There is a story that having this lamp was a major influence on people signing up to rural electrification in Ireland. One wonders if any economist has ever calculated how much the ESB has made over the decades from such lamps burning day and night. Today they are replaced by another red glow 24 hours a day. It is the new God of the TV or stereo standby light.

TOILETS 1954

A little over fifty years ago there was an interesting case reported in the Wexford newspapers.

Many of you will recall the public toilet building at Mann's Lane before the high tech contraption of today was installed. For those who are not aware of the lane heritage, Mann's is the narrow pedestrian lane near Bride Street. Apparently when plans were published to open a public toilet on the site in 1954 there was uproar. It was a bit like halting sites today. Objections were made and an injunction was sought to stop the work. Those seeking the injunction included Mr Pettit who had a grocery store, Mr Radford, a butcher, Purcell's of the pub, Quigley, an electrician and Mr Murphy a teacher who lived locally.

South Main Street: This busy scene on the Main Street probably dates from the 1950s. There is a hoarding up where the public toilets were built in 1954. Traffic is two-way.

As the toilet was built, we must assume that the objections failed. I am surprised that the toilet was only located there for less than fifty years before it was demolished.

Does anyone remember the caretaker of that toilet in the 1960s that had a nickname 'Sugar Al'

IN THE YEAR OF '73

Let's pop back to see how Wexford passed the time in 1973.

At Whites Hotel you could attend a dinner dance and have George Douglas serenade you as you ate and then dance to his music afterwards. The cost was £2-10-0 plus 10%. You were to call Peter Brady or Edward Donovan for a reservation. The Sisters of Mercy were inviting people to view the new school at Kennedy Park. The O'Kennedy School of Ballet was inviting participants for classes in The Long Room at Whites Hotel at the unusual time of 2.10 p.m. on a Saturday. In Jenkins you could hire just about everything for the wedding including dress suits, wedding gowns, bridesmaid's frocks and red carpet. And for after the wedding you could have a system built bungalow for £4000.00. These were prefabricated buildings.

WILLIAMS' ROCK

This was the target of a million Sunday afternoon outings for people of our area.

The rock outcrop was on Whiterock hill and overlooked the later golf course. The full title was 'Jemmy Williams' Rock' but who Jemmy was I haven't a clue. The whole family decamped to the rock early on sunny Sunday afternoons. They brought food, drink, kettles, primus stove, biscuits and rugs. Thinking back it must have looked like a trail of refugees as we tramped excitedly up the steep hill. At Molly Walshe's, a relation of ours, we turned left into a lane at John Conboy's farm where Tommy Daly worked looking after the cattle. The lane led to a house that I seem to recall as unoccupied but we branched off through paths in the briars to the rock. There we set up. The adults sat and talked – took pictures quite often. The youngsters were in a new playground up here – in the country. The field below the rock was a mass of briar and furze with trails worn by hundreds of young feet over the years and we made full use of our imaginations once more. The trips up here were also foraging expeditions. In late summer we came armed with cans and bowls to pick the delicious blackberries for jam and tarts. At other times the quest was for mushrooms in the cattle fields, avoiding the cow pats which we never could.

Picnic on Williams' Rock (Rossiter Collection)

Right: Selskar Abbey Cleanup: Here we see one of the many attempts to clean the grounds of Selskar Abbey. It probably dates from the 1950s with Miss Mai McElroy in the foreground and Kevin O'Mahoney in the background. The lad on the ladder is unknown. (Rossiter Collection)

Below: Gas Car: With petrol rationed during the Emergency this ingenious contraption was fitted to a standard car to operate on gas. We might be looking for the patent again soon. (O'Connor Collection)

Clifford Terrace: This is one of the unique terraces of Wexford built in the late 1800s and into the 1900s. Pay particular attention to the stone column in the middle foreground. It was there to save the wall from the hubs of wagon wheels. (Rossiter Collection)

Talbot Hotel: Here is a view down Trinity Street to the hotel in the 1940s.

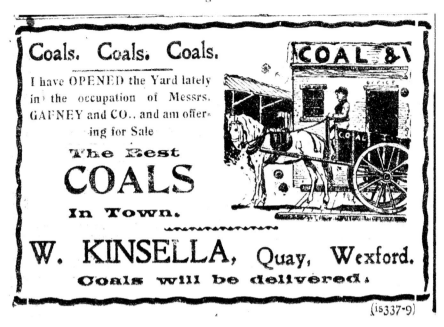

Kinsella Coals – an advert from the early 1900s. (Rossiter Collection)

Maudlintown: This is actually the old Maudlintown. The houses were located opposite the Bishopswater Distillery, now Casa Rio. The slated house to the left survived into the late 1900s and behind a big hedge it was home to the lady who sold the tickets in the Abbey Cinema. (Rossiter Collection)

Above: Pierces Clock noted the beginning and end of the working day for so many Wexford people in decades past. (Rossiter Collection)

Left: JJ Stafford advertised the multi–faceted business. (Rossiter Collection)

THE GUINNESS FESTIVAL CLOCK

For many years the opening of the Wexford Festival Opera, at least for young people, revolved around a mechanical marvel.

Not only were Guinness the major sponsors, they also provided the spectacle of The Guinness Clock to the amusement and amazement of all. The clock was usually located near Wexford's North Station and was a huge attraction for the duration of the Festival. It drew thousands of visitors each year. We were amazed to discover years later that not only was the clock not as unique as we imagined but also we found out it was not a Wexford special – not even an Irish idea.

The first Guinness Clock was put on display in the pleasure gardens at the Festival of Britain. That clock was much larger than the one witnessed by the frozen kneed youngsters of Wexford every October. The original proved extremely popular and all sorts of organizations from town councils to department stores asked to borrow it. In good clear thinking advertising minds this was an opportunity and Guinness had smaller replicas constructed. Now the drinks company was being begged to display their advertising all over Britain.

The first two went to major seaside resorts in 1952. I am not sure how long it took for Wexford to enter the list of venues. Eventually eight clocks were on permanent tour of the British Isles. Apparently the clocks were quite delicate and with so many moving pieces they required a resident maintenance man. Ever the advertising giant, Guinness are said to have had this man counting the numbers mesmerized by the clocks. The clocks toured until the late 1960s and in that year Wexford lost another bit of festival magic.

VII

Myths and Mysteries of Wexford History

Let's take a look back at Wexford in the past and examine some of the myths that have grown up unchallenged over the centuries.

CROMWELL

There is probably no person in our history that gave rise to more myths and mysteries than Mr. Cromwell.

He has been the Stalin, Hitler and Sadam Hussein of Wexford history while being hailed as the sort Martin Luther King of British history. Unfortunately, when a character is so well known we often accept received stories as fact. We do this without thinking.

Did you ever stop to think that in some ways he was the George Bush of 1649? Remember in the 1640s Ireland was seen as a hotbed of persecution of the Protestant faith. Wexford ships harassed the fleets in the Irish Sea and who knows what stories circulated about the 17th century equivalent of 'weapons of mass destruction'.

We are told that when Cromwell arrived at Wexford he placed his guns at Trespan to batter the walls of Wexford. Think about that and look at how far away they would be from the walls. Think of getting big guns up there. Would a gun of 400 years ago have had the range to hit the wall at Barrack Street from Trespan?

Then he got into town. We hear of Stafford's treachery. We connect that to Cromwell's Fort and that Staffords lived there in the 1900s. We add two and two and get six. There was no connection. Many people lived at Cromwell's Fort before Staffords.

Growing up in Wexford there were great tales of that secret tunnel leading from The Friary to the Quay. We loved it. But wait, the friars were killed, why didn't they head off down the tunnel. Oh yes and where was that quay? The current quayside was only built up in the early 1800s, 150 years later. So maybe there was no tunnel.

Then there is the massacre of 2,000 at the market cross. We conjure up a huge 'papal cross type' structure with thousands crammed around it being hacked to death. There is no evidence of such a cross. It was possibly a crossroads where there was a market. It might have been the Bullring. As for 2,000 people killed. Our population was probably not that big in 1649.

Finally let's look at modern Wexford. How many towns have a Hitler Street or a Stalin Road? In Wexford we lived with a Cromwell's Fort for centuries even when attempts were made – usually unsuccessfully - to change street names from monarchs to patriots, the house reminding us of old Oliver remained without any comment. Today his name has spread to drives, courts and avenues and no one bats an eyelid. Are we a tolerant lot or what?

BUFFALO BILL

Buffalo Bill is supposed to have Wexford connections.

Growing up we were told that his Da had been born where Kelly's pub is on the corner of King Street. Unfortunately, despite a recent website I saw recounting this tale; there is no basis for it. Another connection for him is supposed to be Cody's Lane up near The Wicked Swan. Again there is no truth in it even though it would have been great to have a real cowboy from Wexford.

MAIDEN TOWER

While we're up this way let's carry on out the Rosslare Road to Maiden Tower.

Do you remember those tales of the long deep caves under those wonderfully named rocks? I remember many a trip out that way through the fields but never recall entering a cave leading to lost worlds. I do remember some shagging farmers dogs chasing us through furze and gorse though.

I am indebted to Jim Billington for this tale of how Maiden Tower got its name:

'There was a meeting of foxhounds, probably the one which used to meet every Saint Stephen's Day at Kerlogue. Two young ladies were talking while having the Stirrup Cup and one said to the other "How far are you going?" The other young lady replied "Wherever the fox goes I will go." The hunt set off and the fox broke cover and the hounds followed. Eventually the fox headed for the Tower, lost his footing and disappeared over the edge, some of the hounds followed, as did the young maiden. Since then the rock has been known as Maiden Tower.'

Another mystery out that direction was 'The Otter Pond'. Tales of that resounded with stories of it being a bottomless body of water where a person might sink never to be recovered.

DEATH COACH

When you were growing up in Wexford did you ever have the life frightened out of you by tales of the supernatural?

One that I remember was the 'death coach and the headless horseman'. This was supposed to be a bit like The Bow or banshee and foretold a death. Sometime in the late 1950s or early 1960s there was a car accident up near Browne's pub – probably around the corner towards Saint Aidan's. It happened late at night and I must have been too young to be told too much about it but apparently a man was knocked down and killed.

The next morning some of the lads on the street were saying that either they or their Ma had seen the headless horseman and the death coach – a sort of horse drawn hearse – the night before and that was his soul being taken away. Many years later I learned that like all good ghost stories there is an element – sometimes very small – of truth in them.

Back in the late 1700s and early 1800s Wexford like most such towns was awash with malt stores. The rich barley growing areas serviced these and they in turn sent the produce on to Dublin or Bristol. We still have the remnants of some of these either derelict, refurbished as flats – sorry apartments – or waiting to 'fall down' with a bit of developers luck. Like all such successful enterprises the government wanted a few bob out of them and what better way than to slap a tax on the barley. Being cute Wexford farmers of course there had to be a way round coughing up this tax to a foreign power and some of them found it.

Apparently like traffic wardens the tax officials kept fairly regular hours. Maybe not 9 to 5 but they usually slept at night. So the farmers and maltsters hatched a cunning plan. The farmers brought in the barley at night. But there was a problem. The iron-rimmed wheels fairly clattered along rocky roads. The solution was to wrap the wheels in sacking to muffle the sound. Naturally they moved along with little or no lights so if anyone heading home after a 'few scoops' met this horse drawn cart making no sound looming out of the misty dark night they immediately sussed that it was the headless horseman on his death coach.

VIII

Murder in The Bullring

On May 7 1910 Wexford was rocked by a brutal assault that would become a murder case with the death of the victim. At ten o'clock on that Saturday night 18-year-old Mary Anne Wildes was found with her throat cut in a premises in The Bullring.

Simon Bloom aged 29 and of Polish origin rented the studio and apartments above the licensed premises of Philip Keating known as The Cape. Bloom described himself as an artist and canvassed the town and surrounding area selling picture enlargements and frames. His business appeared to be doing very well. He had been in Wexford for about eight years.

Mary Anne Wildes lived with her mother, a widow, at 4 Roche's Terrace. According to early newspaper reports of the time 'the girl to whom he (Bloom) appeared much attached was of humble position'. It was reported that a business relationship was established between them to the extent that when he went to Dublin, 'where he sojourned during the Jewish feast of Passover'; she had the keys and care of his studio.

THE CRIME

On May 7 John Doyle and a companion named Thomas Lewis of Mary Street believed that they heard moaning coming from the hall leading to Bloom's part of the premises. They opened the lid of the letterbox and asked who was there. The voice replied, 'Mary Anne'. The door was locked and the two men tried to decide what to next when they observed Mr Bloom coming from Common Quay Street and heading up the Main Street. They called to him saying there was a child or someone on the stairs. Bloom told them he had left a man and woman inside. He took two keys from his pocket and opened the latch and 'large lock'.

Bullring

On entering the men found a girl leaning against the balusters (banisters?) of the stairs. Bloom shoved her aside to reach the stairs. Aroused she moved towards the door. Blood gushed from a neck wound and 'covered her dress and stained a white rose that she was wearing a dark crimson'. She collapsed in Lewis' arms. Lewis carried the girl out and shouted for someone to fetch a doctor. Some men procured a handcart from a neighbouring public house. The girl was placed on it. Carefully and as quickly as possible they carried her on this cart to the County Infirmary in Hill Street. They took turns pushing the cart while others held handkerchiefs to the wound.

A crowd estimated at about 200 observed the sad procession. These men – John Doyle of Abbey Street, Michael Harpur and Matty Roche of William Street, Michael McMahon of Monck Street, P. Kane of North Main Street and Clem Busher – were later criticised for not waiting for a doctor to attend in the Bullring. At the infirmary Doctor Hadden senior took over.

Miss Wildes was conscious at the time and pleaded that her hair, in which she took great pride, would not be cut. She identified Simon Bloom as her assailant and stated that he had asked her to marry him. She did not indicate what her answer was.

Meanwhile, news of the assault spread through the town. Crowds converged on the building in The Bullring. Walter Busher was sent to the police barracks at George's Street for assistance. People attempting to break in the door were restrained by the arrival of Constables Crawford and Moore who had been on beat duty. Sergeant Scully along with Head Constable McGrath and Constable Abbott soon arrived on the scene from the barracks. The crowd vented angry cries and threats against Bloom and called for the door to be broken in. The officers resisted this and soon a key was procured from Mr Keating the owner of the building.

Mr Corcoran, an employee of Keating, entered the building accompanied by the police officers with the roars of the crowds echoing outside. Stones were thrown and the fanlight on which the name 'S A Bloom' appeared was shattered.

Upstairs the police found Bloom sitting in a chair with a wound to his throat and a letter in his hand. Doctor T Pierce was summoned to care for him. The crowd watched as officers moved from room to room by candlelight. Sergeant Scully recovered a blood stained razor, which he took as evidence.

The crowd continued to grow and reinforcements of police arrived. Father O'Byrne then arrived and called on the crowd 'for the honour of Wexford' to disperse quietly to their homes without bringing 'discredit on the fair name of their town'. The majority dispersed at this appeal but not all. Eventually Reverends T Moran and P Cummins as well as the mayor, R Hanton JP, joined Father O'Byrne and they managed to keep order among a crowd who vowed to remain in The Bullring until the alleged assailant was brought out.

Eventually the people drifted away. The police waited until five o'clock next morning to bring a covered car to the scene and convey Bloom to the Infirmary. At the infirmary he was able to walk to the ward and is said to have enquired as to the condition of 'his girl', Mary Anne Wildes.

VICTIM'S DEPOSITION

On Sunday at 2.30 pm a deposition was taken from the girl. Her condition was so serious that it was thought dangerous to move her to a ward although there was said to be hope she would recover. At the later inquest Doctor Hadden would admit that he 'had no hope for her but I had to tell white lies to try and buck her up.'

The deposition was taken in the surgery of The Infirmary in front of Sir William Paul, resident magistrate. Bloom was carried down from the ward in a bath chair. He had been under constant guard.

Her deposition was:

'I know Simon Bloom who is now present. I am and was acquainted with him. I saw him yesterday at the 6.30 train for Killinick. It was then arranged that I was to visit him at his house in North Main Street. I was in his house last night as arranged. Simon Bloom attempted to choke me'.

Girls: These girls pictured in the familiar Faythe picture of around 1910 give us an indication of the clothing that may have been worn by the murder victim. (Lawrence Collection)

The window blind was then drawn aside to admit better light and permit the girl seeing the accused. Looking at Bloom she added:

'I see Simon Bloom now present and identify him. Simon Bloom attempted to choke me. Simon Bloom caused the injury to my neck.'

Bloom declined to cross-examine her and was formally remanded and returned to the ward.

Miss Wildes' injury was so serious that a special nurse was requisitioned from Dublin. When she arrived in Wexford by the midnight mail train the girl was dead. She passed away at 10 o'clock that Sunday night. The body was taken to the infirmary mortuary to await the inquest. Such crowds gathered as news of the death spread that the police turned out to guard the building.

INQUEST

On Tuesday at 11 o'clock Peter Ffrench, the coroner, opened the inquest in the boardroom of The Infirmary. The following were sworn to the jury; John J Kehoe, Francis Carty, Richard Donovan, Thomas Masterson, Richard Phillips,

Patrick Delaney, John Roche, William Kinsella, William H Allen, Richard Gibson, William J Devereux, Patrick Healy, Joseph Murphy, John Dunne and Mathew Lymberry.

It was 11.35 when they were sworn and viewed the body. Her age was stated as 18 years on the previous October.

Doctor Hadden gave evidence of attending her and finding a wound three inches long above her windpipe. Her clothes including kid gloves were saturated with blood.

George Wildes a tailor employed at Dan Murphy's of Main Street gave evidence identifying his sister. He stated that she left the house, 4 Roche's Terrace, at 8.30 on the Saturday night to go to a boot shop. She was to return within minutes but did not. He gave evidence that she was employed by Simon Bloom from the 25th of the previous month until the 2 May to look after his studio while he was in Dublin. Bloom called to the house on 3 May and asked her to go back into his employment but she refused. George Wildes stated that he was aware of Bloom paying attention to her for about a year but did not know if she resented it or not. He did know that Mary Anne was engaged to Archie Wade, a steward on a merchant vessel. On the previous Thursday Wade told the witness that he was going to marry her.

Further witnesses recalled the incidents on the Saturday night including the fact that Bloom was seen leaving the house and locking the door at 9.50, the witnesses heard the person moaning and called to Bloom who was proceeding past Somers and Porter and away from his house a short time later. They also referred to him trying to conceal the girl from them when he eventually opened his door and referred to getting the man and woman who were alleged to be upstairs.

Brigid Mary Power, a friend of the deceased who was to be her bridesmaid, also gave evidence. She is described in reports as a 'respectably dressed young girl' who lived with her mother at Martinstown. She recalled going to the house on Roche's Terrace at 10 o'clock on Saturday morning and being in the company of Mary Anne Wildes until about 6 o'clock that evening. At 4.30 they had been on the quays as Archie Wade sailed out on the steamer, Wexford, bound for Liverpool. She stated in reply to a question that Simon Bloom had been 'standing in a doorway on the quay while we were there'. As the two girls walked towards Main Street where Power had some shopping to do, Bloom intercepted them in King Street. (The steamer probably left from the ship wharf opposite the present Talbot Hotel). He asked to speak to Wildes in private and Power moved away. She did not hear what they discussed.

Asked if Wildes spoke about Bloom the witness replied that, 'She said he was pestering her and annoying her and that she could not escape him'.

Mary Kate Kearney a carpenter's daughter of Abbey Street gave evidence of seeing the deceased passing Mr Daly's in The Bullring at about 9.30 that evening.

Joseph Edelstien of Dublin addressed the jury with the permission of the coroner. He stated that he was there because, 'the mother and sisters of Mr Bloom came crying and weeping to me and asked me to come and express their sympathy with the family of the deceased girl.' He informed the inquest that in the past weeks Bloom had been totally depressed and heavily in debt.

Sergeant Scully gave evidence that he entered the house (sic) of Simon A. Bloom. He lit a candle on entering and examined the floor and found it covered in bloodstains. In a room upstairs with the words 'Reception Room' on the door he found Bloom reclining in an easy chair. In his hand he found a letter:

'To those who judge us on the scales of humanity and justice – Bull Ring May 7 1910. Are we cowards? We are not afraid to die. Love has conquered fear of death. Are we insane? Is not the heart wiser, more Godly than the mind? Are we lawless? Are we not slaves to our own emotions and swayed by them like a cork in the ocean and powerless to resist? Judge us by them. All those who understands and knows the power and feeling of love, jealousy, circumstances and desperation. We are to be buried side by side. It will not be well for those who disobey this our last and dying wish. May God have mercy on all lost souls.'

After some deliberation the jury returned a verdict that Mary Anne Wildes died as a result of heart failure through loss of blood though a throat wound that in their opinion was inflicted by Simon Bloom.

The foreman went on to praise the actions of the men in procuring a cart and transporting the victim to the infirmary. He said that they gave their evidence intelligently and should be paid for the days work lost in attending the inquest. In an unusual and rather partisan rider Mr Delaney stated, 'It should also be made known that we are sorry such a thing occurred in the town of Wexford and these persons are not natives of Wexford at all.' Presumably he was referring to the alleged assailant.

FUNERAL

The funeral was held on the Wednesday following her death. It took place from her home on Roche's Terrace with large numbers in attendance. The coffin was covered in wreaths. One card read, 'Her soul's flight has reached the heaven's delight' – a sincere friend. There was also a card from Mary and Delia Power stating simply, 'In fond and loving remembrance of our dear Mary.'

The chief mourners were the deceased brothers and Archie Wade of Manchester whom she was to have married in a fortnight. Curiously the newspaper report did not refer to her mother. The cortege moved slowly through the town passing the scene of her attack. The attendance principally included girls of her own age and young women who displayed tokens of mourning.

North Main Street from Bullring: This is the direction Simon Bloom turned before being summoned back to his lodgings. Somers and Porter is the shop on the corner. Philip Cowman, grocer and spirit merchant is next door with a delivery cart outside – similar to that used to convey the victim to the infirmary. Tyler's Shoe store is on the right as is Godkins. (Lawrence Collection)

Simon Bloom who was still under observation at The Infirmary asked to see the remains but was refused as was his request to have a newspaper account of the funeral delivered to him.

THE HEARING

The hearing took place in the boardroom of The Infirmary some days later with Sir William Paul as the presiding magistrate and Mr T J Healy defending Simon Bloom. The formerly clean-shaven Bloom appeared with moustache and curly beard. He appeared calm and sat erect and motionless with his hands placed between his knees.

He was formally charged with 'having on the 7th of May 1910 at Wexford, feloniously, wilfully and with malice aforethought killed and murdered one Mary Anne Wildes.'

Wagons: Wagons like these were a daily feature of the Woodenworks in the 1950s and 1960s as they carried goods to and from the coasters that constantly lined the quays. These were resting behind the railway goods stores. (Rossiter Collection)

Wexford from Clover: Taken in the 1970s on the derelict site of Clover Meats this is a seldom seen view of Wexford. It is interesting in that it shows the gasometer on the left. (Rossiter Collection)

Dated Building: This slate gabled building on the quay was constructed in 1857 as the date shows. (Rossiter Collection)

Rowe's Mill: This is a century old shot of Howard Rowe's Mill. It was located where Redmond Park now stands. (Lawrence Collection)

Towards Charlotte Street: The low building to the left corner of Charlotte Street still exists. Note the railway wagon just under the prow of the ship. The dominant building in the background is probably The Assembly Rooms and houses in John's Gate Street. (Lawrence Collection)

Above: Preparing for the Pikeman Statue: This is The Bullring in the early 1900s. The rounded arches are part of The Tholsel. The person in the cap at the extreme left is probably standing on the railing of the New Market. The street sign to his right refers to Common Quay Street. The sea of caps and bowler hats reflect the fashions of the era. (O'Connor Collection)

Right: The Gas Works: Here we have the nerve centre of the Wexford Gas Consumers Company at Trinity Street. The sign over the door says 'Gas Works Number 5 Yard'. (Lawrence Collection)

Much of the evidence was a repeat of that given at the inquest. But a few new witnesses were called.

Annie Bergin of Gibson's Street recalled meeting the deceased near Cooper's Medical Hall at about twenty past nine on the fateful night. As they conversed Simon Bloom approached and Mary Anne spoke to him for a time and then went with him towards the studio. Bergin said that she went home to Gibson's Street 'with a message' and then met her friend Katie Noctor at the corner of Harpur's Lane. They went for a walk as far as the South Station and back up the quay to Common Quay Street. Walking up Common Quay Street they saw Simon Bloom coming from the Bullring. He turned back and went towards the Main Street. Bergin and Noctor came up to the Bullring as the Town Hall clock struck 10.

Mrs Henrietta Wildes, the mother, then gave evidence. When asked if she knew the prisoner she turned from him saying, 'I don't want to know him. He murdered my child.' When asked if the accused had employed Mary Anne with her mother's consent she replied, 'Yes, he said he would respect her. We know now he respected her grand – to kill her.'

She stated that Bloom had come to the house on 3 May and she went out as he was speaking to Mary Anne at the door. The mother told Bloom that Mary Anne was not going back to work for him and that she was engaged. Bloom said that many an engagement had been broken off. That was at two o'clock. He returned to Roche's Terrace at 9 o'clock and spoke in a room to Mary Anne and Archie Wade. Wade said that she was not to return to his employment. Bloom said that she should have given him a week's notice. Wade said that he would be responsible for that. Mrs Wildes said that Bloom returned again the next day and when he went into room with Mary Anne and shut the door, Mrs Wildes opened it again. Bloom then asked Mary Anne to go to the door with him and she refused.

Bloom provided a written statement to the hearing contained 'in a bulky copy book of eighty-four pages'. The prisoner was formally returned for trial at the next assizes.

REMOVED TO JAIL

The town knew of the hearing taking place but did not know when the prisoner would be moved. After the formal hearing he was removed in a closed cab to the North station by Acting – sergeant Daly and Constable Gallagher. The prisoner stepped from the cab smiling and took his seat in the carriage. A small crowd gathered and watched him but he averted his head. He left Wexford at 4.20 pm on the mail train. There were no demonstrations. Prisoners were usually conveyed via the South Station and a large crowd had gathered there.

An interesting footnote is that when he was leaving The Infirmary, Bloom was served with a Civil Bill for £36 at the suit of a firm in Dublin with whom he carried on business. He threw the writ through the curtains of the cab.

At the subsequent trial Bloom was found guilty and served a number of years in prison for his crime. It is believed that he emigrated to America upon his release. The grave of Mary Anne Wildes is in Crosstown Cemetery and into the present century flowers were regularly place there.

IX

More Miscellany

People seem to love dipping in and out of books. In the previous publication the miscellany section proved extremely popular. In this chapter we pick out a number of short episodes from our past for your amusement and delectation.

DANCING

In 1817 'Mr Garbois, professor of dancing, informed the nobility and gentry that he would give instruction twice a month in Wexford.

All the new Quadrilles and Cotillions, waltzing, and fancy figures would be taught. Applications were to be made at Miss O'Brien's Boarding School, Anne Street'

A hundred years later, the members of the Wexford Commercial Dance Class had a most enjoyable outing to the ever-popular Edenvale. The day was rounded off with a dance at Mrs. Lennon's residence, in which 50 couples participated.

By 1948 dancing appears to have been in disrepute as a protest was made to the Corporation that the jitterbug was nuisance to dancers. This was not because the politicians were authorities on dancing – other than the side step – it was because they owned the dance venue of the Town Hall, now the Arts Centre.

TABLOID TALES

Gruesome as it may be, it is fact that the most popular columns in newspapers are the death notices and crime stories. Here we present a selection from the past.

In 1809 the 3-year-old daughter of Mr Anglin, gun maker of The Quay, fell from upper window on to the street and was killed instantly. In 1841 there were some startling statistics on deaths in Wexford – there were 26 drownings (23male and 3female); 13 people were killed by animals and 16 prisoners (13male and 3 female) died from fever. Inquests showed 2 murders; 5 infanticides; 3 deaths from exposure; 2 suicides; 2 hangings; 4 stabbings and 5 by unspecified causes.

In August 1902 James Walsh collapsed while fishing on quay, having landed a fish. Harbour Constables Morris and Kelly brought him home to Whitemill Road but he died at 4 a.m. next morning.

In a survey of 1887 to determine burial grounds needs for the town, the following was uncovered. 282 people died in the year up to March 1887, this was 23.2 per 1000 of population. 55 died in the Workhouse, 5 in the Fever hospital and 3 the Infirmary. Typhus killed 3; Diarrhoea another 3; Diphtheria accounted for 7 and Measles 1. Bronchitis left 44 dead and pneumonia 2, croup 3; pleurisy 1; congestion of lungs 1 and consumption or TB 35.

In 1831 this notice appeared in the Wexford Independent– 'Whereas the conduct of my wife Eliza Anne Green, alias Tims, alias Weld, has for long been outrageous and vexatious, I am impelled to close my doors against her'. I am not accountable for her debts from September 10th 1831. The aliases indicate that the lady was married at least one before, the first alias being our nee or maiden name.

Then in 1902 – Margaret Anne Hutchinson a shopkeeper, sued Patrick & Mary Malone, of Barrack Street for 17/= owed since November 1901. In the same week Dr Cooper obtained a possession order against Patrick Kehoe of Duke Street. In addition, JJ Percival, secretary of Wexford Loan Fund Society, summoned James Meyler of Barrack Street for sum of 4/9. What was it about Barrack Street a hundred and three years ago?
Setting up business in the past was also an interesting task as this report from 1823 shows.

'Dr Michael Devereux, brother of Dr Nicholas Devereux, informs the public of residing in Wexford after qualifying at University of Edinburgh, he is accepting students to study for 6 years. He is qualified in surgery and midwifery'. There were letters from former patients re-printed in newspaper - John Parle of Clongaddy testified to an operation on a prostate gland that had baffled others and John Pierce from Tacumshane, testified to operation on cancerous tumour at angle of his jaw.

AN EPIDEMIC IN WEXFORD

The cholera epidemic broke out in Wexford in 1832, six years after it first appeared in Bengal, India.

Ten doctors were resident in Wexford at the time and fought the epidemic. The Fever Hospital in what is now Grogan's Road was soon filled and a ship, used to house prisoners during the 1798 rebellion, was commandeered as a hospital and moored in the river Slaney. To keep fever and cholera patients apart, Board of Health hired an unoccupied house at Windmills Hill for fever patients. Locals thought that cholera victims were to be housed and several hundred attacked it. They broke a railing and dipped pieces in a tar barrel and used them to light their way. They threatened to burn the house. Revs Murphy and Hughes Roman Catholic clergymen – remember this was a time when we were part of the empire and newspapers usually distinguished very clearly what denomination was involved - and the police prevented this. Police arrested the ringleaders. Country people were avoiding the town according to the Wexford Chronicle newspaper. When one person became ill, rumours of cholera spread. A number of people tried to take him to hospital by force and the constabulary intervened. The primary victims were the poor living on a diet of cold potatoes, cabbage and sour milk. Burning tar barrels were carried through the town to disinfect air and prevent spread. On board the schooner Maria, 2 of the crew died while she was at the quay, rumours of cholera spread. On February 3rd a letter was sent to pilots from Custom House and Privy Council placing all vessels from the Clyde in precautionary quarantine at anchor in the hale of The Fort of Rosslare. The yellow flag was to be flown when such vessels are being dealt with. In October the worst was over and a notice appeared in the newspapers 'Because of the almost total extinction of cholera in the town a portion of beds were destroyed by fire last Thursday evening. Dr Hannah, Inspector of cholera Hospital left town on October 31st'. Cholera killed 25,000 in Ireland in 1832.

PAUPERS AND WORKHOUSES

A century and a half ago there were 363 paupers listed in Wexford town with 19 in Ardcavan, 15 in Ardcolm and 11 in Artramont.

The board of guardians did their best for such paupers considering the fact that many of those paying towards their upkeep deeply resented them. There is a report in 1854 of the guardians discussing the possibility of buying passage and clothes for two young people named Carty. It would cost £ 4.00 for them to emigrate to New York via Liverpool and there would also be the cost of clothes for the journey. This was weighed against the cost of maintaining them in the workhouse.

In the 1901 census Enniscorthy Lunatic Asylum had 447 patients identified by initials only. Almost all were born in county Wexford. It gave each patient diagnosis and had a Cause of insanity. Here are some interesting ones: Religion, Excessive smoking, Lawsuit, Love Affair, Jealousy, reverse of fortune, pride, effect of foreign climate and quite a few had Drink

THE TWIN CHURCHES OF WEXFORD

On the 27th of January in 1850, within a few short years of the potato famine, a public meeting was held at the Franciscan Church in Wexford.

In the chair was Dr. Myles Murphy, Bishop Elect to the Diocese of Ferns. This meeting was the culmination of 15 years planning by Dr. Murphy. He had been appointed to the parish of Wexford in 1835 on the death of Father Corrin, the man who had pleaded for the lives of both Catholic and Protestant at Wexford Bridge in June 1798.

In the years after that rebellion, Wexford had expanded greatly. Its sailing fleet covered the seven seas and the manufacture of agricultural machinery was growing daily. With this prosperity, the population grew and so did the need for church accommodation.

Dr. Murphy had only been elected bishop some weeks before, but his experience of Wexford drove him to build not a single church, but two. The meeting agreed, Wexford would have twin churches, and the bulk of the task would fall to Father James Roche when he became parish priest 6 months later.

The estimated cost of the buildings was £16,000 each and Father Roche set about raising the money. Every house in the area was canvassed and people were asked how much they could or would pay. Having agreed an amount, arrangements were made and this was collected either in a lump sum or in regular weekly instalments.

In a single week £3,000 was promised. The first instalments were collected on October 12th 1851 and £600 was banked. Over the following 5 years, the full £3,000 was collected in this way. The collection was called The Grand Annual Demonstration and under that name continued for over a century, helping to maintain the churches.

In addition to the Grand Demonstration there was the so-called Chapel Rent. This was the penny or two paid in each and every week by the poorer sections of the community. But it wasn't only local contributions that helped to build the twin churches. Money came from members of all denominations and from Wexfordmen based in all corners of the globe.

An important source of income was the sailing fraternity. These hardy seafarers were perhaps the ones most conscious of the growing churches. As they returned from voyages to Africa, America or The Black Sea, their eyes would scan the horizon as they entered Wexford Harbour. There on the skyline, they would see the progress as the twin spires grew. Then, before going ashore to family and friends after a six-month voyage, the hat was passed around. The collection was made for 'the canon' as Father Roche was known, and sailors thankful for a safe voyage were generous. The account books are littered with references to such contributions, from The Petrel, The Falcon, The Helen and many others. Year after year the money rolled in - the pounds from the rich, the shillings of the workers and the pennies of the poor.

In 1854 Father Roche was advertising in the newspapers for anyone with subscriber cards to forward them without delay. These were the subscriptions for the twin churches, which were only two years from opening.

The churches opened for worship in 1858. By 1881 over £52,000 had been collected and spent on the twin churches planned 30 years before.

An existing letter shows both the humour and persistence of Father Roche, which made this mammoth task a reality. It is addressed to a Mr. Murphy of Clonard, who was having a bit of luck with the horses but apparently forgetting about the churches.

It reads: 'Dear Murphy, You have won two races without giving me a donation, so now make up, Most Faithfully Yours, James Roche P.P.'

IN THE 1850S

In the year 1852 there was an interesting competition held at The Mechanics Institute in Wexford.

Surgeon Lover gave a series of lectures on electricity that year and the committee decided to hold a quiz in conjunction with the series. Twenty-one people came forward for examination including three girls. The questions were printed on cards and three cards were given to each contestant. Anyone failing to answer one of the three questions dropped out. This continued until the number was down to five.

These included Margaret Codd who would later become Reverend Mother of the Convent of Mercy in London and found a House of Refuge there. Patrick Kavanagh who would become a friar was there. William Murphy who later became master of The Enniscorthy Workhouse was still in the running as was Nathaniel Vicary who would join the Royal Navy. The fifth contestant was Master North.

Vicary and Murphy received silver medals. Miss Codd was awarded a set of books, as were Kavanagh and North.

It is interesting to note the presence of the ladies at lectures and quizzes at a time when most people thought the fair sex were discounted in educational pursuits.

There was an advert in the local papers for maintenance of what was called The Free Bridge from The quay to Ferrybank that would cost £ 220.00. This reminds us of two things. The oak bridge – scene of executions in 1798 was now toll free and also the bridge at Carcur was not yet built – it was to open in 1856.

The Wexford Archers Club was advertising a meeting in Whites Hotel.

The Sewed Muslin Company brought a girl to court and sued her for keeping a piece of muslin. This was part of the practice of out-working which was common to industry and essential to boosting family incomes at the time. The company would provide pieces of muslin and women and girls would sew it up in their homes for what were often meagre earnings.

In a sort of Situations Wanted column, a man advertised for a position as a butler. He informed potential employers that he had been 20 years with Mr Hore of Harperstown. Anyone interested in employing him was asked to contact Mr Walker the grocer or Mr Walpole of Westgate.

GRAVEYARD CONSECRATION

In the 1880s the order was made to close the old town cemeteries in Wexford. This caused considerable protest but people eventually accepted the reasons – overcrowding and sanitation worries.

On Sunday, 1 May 1892, Bishop Browne performed the ceremony of consecration the grounds of the Roman Catholic section of Crosstown Cemetery. This was the first time in centuries that such a ceremony was witnessed in the town as all the older cemeteries dated back into history. Accompanied by the mayor and corporation members he proceeded to a mound in the centre of the cemetery where a large wooden cross was erected. There he blessed the holy water for the ceremony.

Large crosses were placed on the four sides of the cemetery and three lighted candles placed at each. Having recited special prayers at each site he moved these candles to the arms and head of the cross where they were fixed. Benediction was then celebrated at the main cross for the thousands who attended the historic ceremony.

On 3 May Reverend Doctor Packenham Walsh, Bishop of Ossory and Ferns consecrated the Protestant section of the ceremony.

CONSUMPTION 1903

In March 1903 Consumption or Tuberculosis was rampant in Ireland. As part of the health education regarding the disease advertisements were placed in local newspapers.

'Consumption is not usually inherited but some children are born with a constitution that favours their catching it.'

'Intemperance, overcrowding, the stuffy air of unventilated rooms, dirty, damp or dark dwellings are among the causes which render people liable to consumption.'

Precautions: A consumptive person must NOT spit on the footpath or the floor of any room, railway carriage, tramcar, cab etc. Such person should neither swallow the spittle nor allow it to be smeared on the bedclothes, beard or wearing apparel. He should cover his mouth with the hand in the act of coughing and those who live with him should avoid too close contact when a bout of coughing occurs.'

'A consumptive should NOT sleep in the same bed as another person.'

'Keep windows open as much as possible. Spit into a handkerchief or a cup containing some water or a spitting flask out of doors. Floors should be swept with wet tea leaves.'

HOUSE SALES

In the early years of the twentieth century, people were very open about property sales and the prices paid.

One such auction was reported having taken place in the Town Hall by order of the Lord Chancellor for Ireland selling part of the estate of Mr. Paul Joseph Carroll. It was sold in 19 lots.

Three houses in Keyser's Lane and two in Gibson Street held under lease for the life of the Duke of Connaught and let to five weekly tenants. Bought by James Furlong, rate collector, South Main Street for £50.

House in Lower Bride Street, let to James McMahon at a weekly rent. Purchased by Mr. McMahon for £70.

Seven houses in Carrigeen Street and Bride Place let to weekly tenants. Purchased by Mrs Anastasia Keating of Carrigeen Street for £560.

Two houses in John Street let to weekly tenants – purchaser, Mrs Boyle of John's Gate Street for £80.

Three houses in Cornmarket held under fee farm grant. Let to one yearly and two weekly tenants. Bought by James Furlong, rate collector, South Main Street for £160.

Two further houses in Cornmarket bought by same man for £75.

The swan: This is a familiar picture but we include it because with some enhancement we noticed that some chickens appear in front of the houses in the centre of the picture where a young child (it could be male or female in that era) appears at the door in an apron. Note also the shutters on the windows. (Lawrence Collection)

Above: Towards Charlotte Street: The low building to the left corner of Charlotte Street still exists. Note the railway wagon just under the prow of the ship. The dominant building in the background is probably The Assembly Rooms and houses in John's Gate Street. (Lawrence Collection)

Opposite above: Boys in the Bullring: This picture is late 1800 or early 1900. The Tholsel wall is visible with the fountain attached. Many people thought of the fountain here when it was called 'fountain square' as an ornate Italian style construction. The ass and carts may have delivered good Rosslare Herrings for the fish sellers. One such lady is visible to the right. (Lawrence Collection)

Two houses in Charlotte Street let to weekly tenants again bought by James Furlong for £120.

Part of the lands at Coolcotts containing about 2 roods with a dwelling house thereon – was purchased Wm Maddock for £60.

Catherine O'Neill of North Main Street purchased House in Monck Street, for £95.

House in Monck Street purchased by Patrick Furlong, Abbey Street, for £100.

James Furlong purchased two houses in Keyser's Lane for £50.

James McMahon P.L.G. purchased House in Lower Bride Street, let to Mrs Elizabeth McMahon for £50.

Five houses in Castle Hill Street purchased by James Furlong at £500.

Mrs Cullen of William Street purchased House in William Street with small garden on the opposite side of William Street for £60.

Two houses in Bride Place purchased by John Nolan of Wygram for £90.

Two houses in John Street and two in Francis Street were bought by Miss Hayes of Cornmarket for £300.

Mrs Boyle of John's Gate Street bought three houses in Wygram Place for £85.

One house in Slaney Street and two in Temperance Row were purchased by Mrs Catherine O'Neill of North Main Street for £75.

James Furlong, rate collector, bought two houses in Abbey Street for £60.

Above: The Crescent: The horses outnumber the lorry in this picture, probably from the 1950s. The cart in the foreground is loaded with hempen sacks probably containing corn or barley. The whitewashed building with the pointed gable was a forge where horses were shod in the late 1950s. I think a Mr Malone operated it. It later house 'Bookends' where we bought our second-hand books. You will notice that the rear entrance to the present Penney's had more than a mere arch at the time.

Left: Cornmarket in the 1940s: Only the Thomas Moore Tavern, in the far left is familiar in this streetscape. Even then there was demolition taking place to the left of it. This picture is interesting for the lovely shop fronts in the centre and two poles just feet apart. The small paned windows up closer are of particular note.

Hill Street: This is a view of upper Hill Street around 1917.

Hill street 1917: This section from the Redmond funeral shows the south side of
Hill Street. The Gaol is in the right background. The houses on the right were later
demolished. It is interesting to note the few people watching the funeral.

CRIME IN 1917

When Barbara Berry of Stonebridge Lane died after being stabbed, her children Johanna and Anne were committed to the Industrial School.

They were sent to Good Shepherd School in New Ross. Sergeant Collopy stated that he found only a single bed in the family home for the father and five children. Called 'a little girl', Mary O'Grady of Carrigeen was accused of stealing boots from Mr Donovan's shop on consecutive days. Robert Coffey, pawnbroker, stated that he had accepted two pairs of boots from the girl. On hearing of the missing boots he sent for the girl and her mother. When they did not arrive he informed the police.

Her father stated that Mr Coffey should not take goods from a child under 14. Mr Coffey said she told him she had passed 14 last year. He stated that 'her people are a small race'. The magistrates fined her 10/= but stated their belief that shop-keepers displaying goods outside were offering temptation.

WEXFORD BUSINESSES

Let's have a quick look at business in Wexford in 1922.

The Roche Brothers of Castlebridge announced that they had purchased the drapery business of J.E. O'Reilly as a going concern. They were looking forward to seeing customers at 60 North Main Street. The brothers included the father of Mary who later married Joe Bailey of New Ross and started a butchers business in Bridge Street that is still open. Joe was a great GAA player and supporter and they had the finest rocking horse in Ireland on their landing for Anne and Dick – and visiting cousins from Wexford.

People Newspapers were offering printing of admission tickets and of cheque books in Irish or English.

Charles Rowe was offering a Ford two-seater – owner driven and not much used – for £ 135. If you only wanted to hire a car, J.J. Bell of The Old Pound and Thomas Street was your man.

John Sinnott & Co announced the opening of a workshop at St. Peter's Square for cabinet making and funeral undertaking.

At Haddens you could get what they described as 'a well cut hand made lounge suit' for only £ 4-15-0. For the ladies they had Derby Boots and patent leather walking shoes.

Still with fashion, Healy and Collins offered Jazz Jumpers for 8/6, coat frocks for 21/6 and also golf coats at very tempting prices.

Thompson Brothers offered a Fordson tractor for £ 120.

Patrick Donovan of Crescent Quay was selling house coal at 44/= a ton. You could order by telegram to Donovan Shipowner.

Jobs on offer included 'a good general servant for a farmer's place' at £ 18 a year. Another person wanted a 'general man, single, for a country rectory'. He should be able to milk, care for a horse and trap and do plain gardening. There were lots of adverts for parlour maids and cooks so the relics of ould decency were obviously thriving.

Howard Rowe & Co. offered nutty brown bread for sale and Cousin's Mineral Waters and licensed Wine Brewers had Grape Wine from the finest concord grapes at 2/8 a bottle. Cousins also entreated people to buy Wexford Dry Ginger Ale and other table waters rather than pay higher prices for inferior products from Dublin. Mr Murphy of 10 Lower John Street would repair your accordion, concertina or violin bow.

FATHER GAUL'S

Ask any Wexford person of a certain age about boys clubs and depending on which end of town they come from or which extreme of the age range you will get one of two answers.

The people with roots in the south end and Bishopswater area and aged in their fifties downwards will say Father Sinnotts or The Josephs. Get the North Enders aged fifty upwards and unequivocally it will be Father Gaul's. They seldom give a saint's name but in fact this earliest boy's clubs in Wexford was officially known as St Vincent's Boys Club.

The official opening of this club took place in Selskar in the 1930s. The premises were blessed by Fr Butler assisted by Fr O'Neill, director of the Legion of Mary and Fr Gaul the spiritual director and founder of the club. They referred to the purpose of the club as the physical well being of the boys of the town.

The boys were then entertained to tea catered by the ladies of the Legion of Mary. Games then included musical chairs and blind boxing. The club was open two nights each week offering table tennis and rings. It was hoped to employ a gym instructor too. The club was for boys aged 14 upwards.

Ask them where Father Gaul's went on the very special summer camp and many will reply Carne. In later years they are right but at least in 1937 they decamped in the opposite direction. Yes in that year St Vincent's Boy's Camp was at our own Curracloe. The camps were an institution in Wexford in those days long before the package holiday to the costas. Boys – the girls seemed to have been relatively neglected – usually from working class areas where the luxury of holiday could not even be contemplated were treated to one or two weeks under canvas at the seaside.

Above left: Fire Lighters: This is an old advertisement for locally made firelighters almost a century ago. Look at the advertising copy writing. They even costed the price per fire. (Rossiter Collection)

Above right: NJ Cullen: Cullen was a top bicycle emporium in old Wexford. This advertisement is interesting for the bicycle lamps on offer from electric run on a dynamo or battery to acetylene. Many will ignite memories in former cyclists. (Rossiter Collection)

In 1963 the club moved to Green Street and occupied the premises of Saint Michael's Club and officially opened its doors on December 1st.

BACK IN 1939

In 1939 Stanley Hayes of The Bullring was prosecuted for having people on the premises at 9.50 pm on a Saturday night.

Guard Traynor found the men in The Cape snug. Mr Hayes stated in court that he had trouble getting them to leave. He and his assistant already had their coats and hats on. The publican got off but the drinkers were fined 2/= each.

Owen Kehoe of Selskar was in court for having four men drinking at 12.50 on a Sunday. He said he had agreed to let them in on his return from Mass. The publican pleaded that it was a wet day and the men had called to see if he was going to a match. The charges under the Sheebeen Act were adjourned.

At the Imperial Bar owned by MJ Kavanagh there were a number of people caught. One stated that he had been playing cards upstairs with Miss Wickham and Miss Walsh and just happened to be leaving as the guards arrived. The others were stated to have been guests of a Mr Sullivan - a bus company official but having a drink constituted an offence. Again the fines were 2/= each.

The *Menapia* brought a dredger to Wexford on her first voyage in 1939. Another *Menapia*, a steamer, had arrived in Wexford in 1892 and was visited by thousands.

COTTAGE DANCE

In May 1939 Mrs Connors of Killabeg, Ferns appeared in court charged with permitting her Board of Health cottage to be used for a public dance. In court it was stated that she lived in the cottage with her two children and her lodger with his wife and two children. A number of people attended but she did not charge admission. One lady brought tea, sugar, a loaf, biscuits and sugar. Another brought bread, tea and butter. She provided tea for the crowd. She said she had intended to have a game of cards but did not do it because she was told she needed a licence. She was fined £10.

Wexford Corporation agreed to pay an extra penny an hour when involved in dirty work. This included working in any old dirty sewers, cleaning silt from sewers clogged by silt from factories and cleaning The Horse River. A plan to provide long boots was held up because special licences were required to import them.

ADVERTS IN 1939

Henry Hogan & Son announced the opening of General Blacksmiths workshops at Batt Street for plain and artistic gates and railings plus repairs to all classes of agricultural machinery and wheel-binding and cart work.

Cousins & Co offered tonic water in siphons.

R G Stoker of Tinahealy offered three ferrets for 25/= the lot. You could have the hutch if you could carry it away.

R Breen on the Quay offered bedsteads complete with wire mattress for just 20/=. A fibre mattress would cost 15/=. There were also offers on hair mattresses and bolsters. Mattresses could be re-teased and made as new.

P.J. O'Connor could supply anything from cake tins to storm lamps to plough parts from his North Main Street shop.

At Cooke's Sporting Depot at 77 North Main Street you had guns of all descriptions with cartridges and accessories.

Healy & Collins: this was one of our important department stores in the mid 1900s, before the national names began to dominate. Look at the marketing ploy of refunding travel costs and the fact that extra trains were laid on for Christmas Shopping. (Rossiter Collection)

Bullring: Here is the Bullring in the mid-twentieth century. The Cape is advertising Capstan cigarettes. There is plenty of parking. The Tholsel has not been demolished.

Remember bringing parcels home on the bike? At Cullen's there were carriers with spring clips and straps - in Selskar. They also offered HMV records - songs, dance and comedy at 1s 10d.

Walsh and Sons in Cornmarket offered saddles of every description and paid top price for horsehair and feathers.

A full pint size bottle of stout would set you back 10d at Tom Kehoe's 21 Selskar Street.

Jack Fane was offering whiskey - not a bottle less than 10 years old stocked at 38 North Main Street.

In New Ross, Fleming's of North Street had delicious teas - for that brighter outlook.

Coopers Medical Hall advertised 'The Wexford Cough Cure' - Dr Firths - guaranteed to break up the worst coughs in 48 hours.

Haddens were offering 2/6 in the pound off. A matrons costume would cost 63/= and men's suede twill pyjamas went for 5/6.

We had interesting tastes in 1939. L&N offered Canary Tomatoes, Dried Figs, Stoneless Dates at 17 South Main Street.

People were less squeamish in 1939. There were front-page adverts for hearses, coffins and habits.

Rochford Drapers offered Waterproof Riding Coats with straps, saddle pieces etc. You could also have breeches made to order and silk sports handkerchiefs.

BACK IN 1943

Radio was the mass media source back in 1943 and Wexford was featured on 9 September on the national airwaves. This was a broadcast of a celebrity concert by the Wexford Theatre Guild, director John Welsh – yes Welsh not Walsh.

The stars were James McCafferty, baritone, Moira Griffith, soprano, Hugh Maguire, violinist and accompanist Charles Maguire. The venue was the Town Hall and patrons were warned that they could not enter or leave the concert between 8 and 10 by order of the broadcasting authorities.

On the water Jack Lett of Batt Street and his crew went to the rescue of the 'Maura' belonging to Chris Hopkins in the North Bay in 1943. The boat had lost power and had to be towed in heavy seas. The rescuers included Jack Lett, John Lett, William Duggan and Larry Hayes.

At a Labour Party meeting in Castlebridge there was discussion as to whether women could become members of the men's branch or if they should open their own branch. Obviously it was a hard choice and a decision was left to a later meeting.

We should note that in the period we are looking at there was no bridge in Wexford town. The county council members came up with the idea of as they called it a 'floating ferry' – what other kind was there. As usual they had a bicker about costs. The harbour board would not finance it for one reason they said and the corporation would not do it for another.

Then the county manger remarked that if they handed it over to an energetic young fellow he could retire before they had the bridge built in about five years. As it turned out it was fifteen years later before it opened so three energetic young fellows could have made their fortunes.

Let us relive the Leaving Certificate success of those who achieved honours in the exam back in 1943 at St Peter's College. They were Laurence Murphy, John Roche, James Wall, Thomas White and James K. Kelly. Yes that is the full Honours List. Subjects included Latin, Greek, Algebra and Geometry. The latter two are now part of Maths but were separate subjects then.

What were people buying in Wexford in 1943?

Con Macken at The Cape offered best drinks as usual but also advertised pure ground coffee at 3/= a pound, raisins at the keenest prices and fresh butter bought daily.

Hanton's established in 1812 offered coffins in oak, elm, pitch pine and deal. You could have a motor or horse drawn hearse. Mind you Boggan's offered a Rolls Royce hearse.

The cinemagoers were in for a shock as The Capitol and Palace cinemas advertised a price increase due to higher cost for films.

E. Marcus an eyesight specialist from Dublin was on tour offering free eyesight testing and glasses from 21/=. He was to visit The Globe Hotel in New Ross, Bennett's Hotel in Enniscorthy, Kelly's Hotel in Newtownbarry – Bunclody for the younger readers, The Traveller's Hotel in Gorey.

We were told that Aspro offered a good night's sleep and Fynnon Salt relieved leg pain.

The government published a list of maximum prices that goods could be sold for.

Fresh milk was available bottled or loose. Biscuit varieties included Square Meal, Kerry Cream, Arrowroot and Jam Puff. Household candles were offered in 14 sizes and cigarettes had to be sold in multiples of 5.

Firewood blocks could not exceed 10 inches in diameter.

Petrol was to cost 3/1 from the pump per gallon but a penny more in cans.

Turf was sold for 64/= a ton or 3d for a dozen sods.

John Street: This appears to have been a popular streetscape in Wexford a century ago. The Lawrence Collection features it but this shot is from the Valentine Collection. (Valentine Collection)

North Main Street from Selskar: This wonderful picture appears to date from around the 1950s as evidenced by the children's clothing. The shops have changed hands since then. Fennell's appears to be selling toys and fancy goods. The next shop front is illegible but then comes Larkin's followed by Gaynor's. Across Monck Street on the corner is Doran's offering hardware, china and fancy goods and with a 'Players Please' hoarding on the billboard. O'Connor's comes next. On the right hand side is Griffin's turf accountants. The man accompanying the other with the hat appears to be in a shop coat. (O'Connor Collection)

The Crescent with Boats: it is difficult to date this picture. There is a gas light on the quay but it may be just a reminder of times past. The cranes appear to be in working order. The boats are laid up for painting and repair. The level of the walk around the Crescent is higher and more uneven than at present. (Rossiter Collection)

The Quay: This picture of a century ago shows the working quay. There is a paddle steamer on the right with goods being loaded or unloaded. On the woodenworks are the railway wagons. Then comes the railway line and the crates beside it. The lighting is still gas. On the south corner is 'The Provincial Bank of Ireland' a building that still stands as part of Wexford Credit uUion. (Lawrence Collection)

North Main Street: This is reproduction from a postcard. The shop on the near right is Walkers. Further on is a bicycle shop offering the wares of Singer and Enfield Bicycles. They also sell Pratt's Spirit. Next door you could buy 'the best makes of cigars, tobaccos and cigarettes'. Then is The Seed Warehouse and beyond that is a sign that looks like a clock but is a circle. The light jutting out from the building on the left advertises White's Hotel. (Lawrence Collection)

Ferrycarrig: This view shows horse and carts conveying sacks towards Wexford. The railway embankment, wall and road at this point have changed little in a hundred years. (Lawrence Collection)

AND 25 YEARS BEFORE THAT!

A house at Dempsey's Terrace in Wexford was sold £700 to Miss Banville of Assagart. The seller was Nicholas Rossiter – no I'm not that old.

A seaside property with a thatched roof and 8 acres of land at Ballyconnigar, Blackwater was sold by Julie Corrigan to J. Armstrong of Enniscorthy for £225.00.

Blackberries were fetching 3 shillings a stone in Ballymurn.

Glynn Pioneers held their annual outing to Kilmore Quay.

At a talent contest in Kilmore winners included Mrs Jeffries of Neamstown, James Magee and Sheila Keating of Bridgetown.

James O'Connor of Wolfe Tone Villas was the owner of the only pigeon to arrive home from Larne.

1944 BITS

Back in 1944 there was a Wexford School of Acting at the Theatre Royal.

Rita and her band advertised for engagements – terms moderate. This was Rita Redmond of St Johns Avenue.

Martin Crosbie was appearing at Theatre Royal as guest star in Variety on Parade.

Anew McMaster would be on the following week with seven plays including Jane Eyre and *Oedipus the Tyrant*.

The Hope and Anchor Bar opened at 73 South Main Street with John Tyghe proprietor.

Coffeys were selling army boots at 15/= a pair.

Ely House contents were for sale by direction of Major General Doran.

There was a fine art and antiques sale at Johnstown Castle.

Mr AKS Roche was selling Clifford House at Rosslare Harbour.

There was a grand entertainment in The Theatre Royal with the HFC band and a local services pageant. This included a music programme with soloist Nellie Walsh; ballet with a troupe under Mrs Kavanagh; Irish Dancing by St Michaels Boys Club under Mr J Sharkey.

The Pattern was held at John's Street Graveyard.

Fuel Importers advertised a tender the construction of a 'rubble road' through the turf dumps at Kirwan's Field.

Wexford Development Association ran a Market Train from Waterford every Saturday arriving at 11.45 and returning at 5.00.

Patrick Whelan announced the purchase of Rochfords at 12 NMS for grocery and bar - two new lounge bars added. To be called 'The Irish House'. Open 9.30 am to 10 pm.

Shaw's at 87 North Main Street announced closure.

ARDCAVAN RACES

In 1900 the long defunct races on the North slobs at Ardcavan had been revived thanks to the efforts of well-known local solicitor MJ O'Connor and a committee of local business people.

On Friday September 14 1900 it was a fine day and the town was in festive mood and many people relished a trip to the races. With the nearest land crossing at Carcur, local boatmen were only too pleased to cash in on the event and they did a roaring trade ferrying passengers across directly from the quays.

One such boat was *The Dolphin*. It ferried people directly from the Woodenworks. At Ardcavan, with no quay or slipway, they were taken ashore is a smaller boat which was towed behind. This boat was crewed by John Coles of Byrnes Lane and Alec Swan of William Street.

The first group of passengers crossed the harbour and was ferried safely to shore. At about 1 pm another twenty-two passengers crowded into this small boat for that final short journey. Such was the eagerness of punters to get to the races that many had to be forcibly restrained from boarding. The small craft cast off from the 'Dolphin' in bright sunshine and still water. Despite the ideal conditions water began to spill into the boat. This caused people to panic. Men, women and children milled about causing further water to pour in. The boat began to sink.

People standing on the slob embankment and remaining passengers on the Dolphin stared in shocked disbelief. They were friends and relatives of those in the floundering boat. As the water was only 5 to seven feet deep it was felt that all that would be suffered was a wetting. Two other boats rushed to the scene and hauled people aboard.

Amazingly, in shallow water, close to shore and with hundreds of on-lookers, seven people disappeared beneath the waves. Despite valiant efforts no bodies were found on the day. Wexford fell into deep mourning. Friends and relatives scoured the shore into nightfall.

On Saturday three bodies were recovered but still there was no sign of the others. It took a falling tide on Sunday for the other four to be spotted and taken from the water. The seven who died were:

Denis and Catherine Kenny of Patrick's Square – their six-year-old daughter Mary was one of those rescued. Two other children had stayed at home on the day. Mary Furlong of William Street – she had just become engaged and had travelled to the races with her fiancée, her parents, a brother and sister. William

Duggan of Carrigeen – he left a wife and six children. Patrick Doyle of Distillery Road – a Gaelic Footballer with Mulgannon Harriers. William and Martin Blake, two brothers from The Faythe – William worked in Howard Rowe's Mill while Martin was a sailor. Martin had ironically just returned from two years on the high seas to drown in the calm waters of his native harbour.

As was usual in that time the inquest was opened on the Monday at the courthouse. The jurors were sworn and in what may appear gruesome to modern sensibilities but was the standard practice of the time they were then brought by carriage and visited each of the victims' houses to view the bodies. The members of the jury were: John Fitzsimons, Main Street (foreman); Matthew O'Connor, Main Street; Ald. NJ Cosgrave, Selskar; Michael Nolan, Main Street; James Sinnott, Thomas H. Richards, Bull Ring; RH Shaw, Main Street; Richard Young, Main Street; John Doyle Captain Patrick Kelly, Main Street; John P. Rochford, Main Street; James Stafford, Main Street; Michael Kelly, Monck Street; James O'Leary, Main Street, and George Daly, Bull Ring. The names will be familiar to anyone who has looked at the businesses of Wexford at the time. Like voting, jury service was the preserve of the elite.

The first witness heard was John Furlong of William Street, Wexford, a sailor. He was the father of one of the victims, Mary Furlong. Patrick Gordon, brother-in-law of Denis Kenny, was next then Martin Murphy, The Faythe, and James Roche, Batt Street, a fish and poultry dealer followed him. James Roche told the inquest that he left Wexford quay at 12 o'clock on the day in question on board the Dolphin, with Captain James Swan in charge.

After the Dolphin anchored, about 12 or 14 people got into the small boat and they were put ashore. The next group included the people who were drowned. When asked to describe how the accident occurred, he said:

'She gave a bit of a lurch and came back, and the next time she gave a lurch to the land side and she went down.'

The Coroner asked, 'Were there too many people in the boat?'

The witness replied, 'She had about a foot of water to spare in the centre, and about a foot and a half fore and aft.'

'What happened after that?'

'The next thing was trying to save the people.'

Before the inquest was adjourned, the evidence of Moses Boggan, The Faythe, a master mariner, who had been a passenger in the Dolphin, was taken. He told the inquest that there were about 60 people on board the Dolphin. After the Dolphin anchored, he got into the small boat with 13 others and got safely ashore.

'The small boat then went back to the Dolphin for a second load. I immediately went up to the racecourse.' Moses Boggan said that in his view, it would not have been prudent for the Dolphin to go closer to shore. When he was asked about people jumping into the small boat, he told the inquest, 'you would need a gun to keep them out.'

So it was a little over a century ago that Wexford lost seven people in her calm sunlight harbour.

THE BRIDGES OF WEXFORD

We go back a little more than two centuries to the first major bridge over the Slaney at Wexford to directly link Castlebridge to the town.

Up until then the crossing was by ferry from Ferryboat Lane. This was a part of land given by Cromwell to General Monck along with the ferry rights. His family intermarried with Grogan's of Johnstown and for many decades they controlled the crossing of people and goods to Castlebridge. With the improvements and expansion of the town and trade it was agreed that a bridge was needed and a committee of shareholders was formed because at that time you needed an act of parliament to institute such undertakings.

'A meeting held on 2nd day of June, 1794, convened by public notice, for the purpose of determining the site of the bridge, intended to be built of the River Slaney.' A committee of nine was named to act for the entire committee, and an act of Parliament (33 Geo. III) was obtained to authorize the commissioners, as they were called, to erect the bridge. An ingenious American, Mr. Lemuel Cox, was contracted with to carry out the intention of the commissioners for the sum of £15,000.

Cornelius Grogan was the chairman and among the shareholders investing that total of £ 15,000 was – Right Hon. Marquis of Ely, (Robert Hughes, Esq.), Cornelius Grogan, Johnstown, Beauchamp Bagnell Harvey, Thomas Grogan Knox, John Grogan, Ebenezer Jacob, Narcissus Huson, Arthur Meadows, Miller Clifford, William Kearney, Patrick Prendergast, Rev. William Eastwood, John Johnstone, John Connick, Ambrose Hughes, John Lightburn, Patrick Keating, Miss Mary Corish, Nathaniel Hughes, John Cullimore, Thomas Jones, William Archer, Robert Maylor (Meyler?), William Devereux, John Pettit, John Colclough, James Harvey, Richard Neville, William Hatton, John Cardiff, Matthew Hughes, Christopher Richards, Loftus Richards, Richard Waddy, MD., John Couzons (Cousins), Henry Hatton Gird, Richard Gainfort, William Hughes, Charles Stanley Monck, Miss Bridget Corish, Miss Margaret Corish, Matthew Keugh (Keogh), Andrew Rock, Mrs. Dorothy Archer, Mrs. Fisher, Christopher Taylor, Arthur Leared, Thomas Richards, John Redmond, Mrs. Eliza Hatton, Robert Sparrow, Nicholas Sinnott, Robert Carty, Nicholas Dixon, Mrs. Mary Hobbs, Miss Hatchell, William Boxwell, John Hay, George Lacy, Anthony Lee, James E. Devereux, & Miss Marianne Carty. All spellings are as in the original documents.

It is interesting to note that of the shareholders there were a number of ladies investing quite substantial sums. In fact Miss Hatchell was one of only two invest-

Above: South Main Street at Fettitt's Lane: The shop on the left offers paints, window glass and wallpaper and advertises as an agent for 'Pullars Dye Works Perth'. Byrne's is on the right and what appears to be Harris next door. Leverette & Frye are 'grocers and agents for W & A Gilbey' on their advertising with the gas lamp. There is a fine pony and trap parked outside. (Lawrence Collection)

Left: White's Hotel (Lawrence Collection)

Bottom of George's Street: On some old maps this building is referred to as The Magazine. It may be connected to the constabulary barracks that was located in George's Street but it is more likely allied the artillery park referred to in a map circa 1800 and located at the bottom of Slaney Street. (O'Connor Collection)

George's Street: This is where O'Connor's Solicitors red brick building later stood. It is believed to have been the townhouse of Bagenal Harvey. (O'Connor Collection)

My Wexford

The Pump House: This is a modern photograph of the pump house at the North Slob. (Rossiter Collection)

ing £ 1000.00, she may have been a member of the family who owned Hatchell's Bank that was operating in Wexford at the time. Of the other names mentioned Hatton and Ely were substantial landowners with the former still being recognised into the late twentieth century owning houses or land in the town. Another feature of the names is that many of the surnames still occur in the town while some of the more exotic have disappeared.

The man employed to erect this magnificent oak bridge was Lemuel Cox, an American. When we consider that our present bridge is one of the longest in the country we realise the mammoth engineering feat taken on over two centuries ago.

The oak bridge was 1554 feet long and 34 feet wide. To build it, 75 piers of oak, each with six timbers had to be driven into the harbour bed. In addition it needed a portcullis so that shipping would be able to proceed upriver. In fact the notes state that even at low tide there was a depth of water known as a draught of 16 feet.

Apart from being an engineering feat the bridge was also a thing of beauty. It has Chinese railings, two orchestra points in the centre with recesses and seats offering shelter. The bridge was a fashionable promenade where the gentry took their strolls and the bands attached to the military units stationed in Wexford frequently played on the bridge. This was a working bridge with tolls and these repaid the shareholders handsomely over the years.

The shareholders were not fools and decided that the bands were not charged the toll but the promenaders had to pay. In 1807 the toll company, which changed in a sort of franchise every three years, decided to charge the Tyrone Militia Band. Their commander moved them off the bridge and we may presume that they played elsewhere in Wexford and probably drew some toll paying promenaders away from the bridge. In 1831 for hay auction at Artramont near Castlebridge the company had the bridge declared toll free for purchasers from town side of river

Disaster struck in October 1827 when the centre portion collapsed. There is no report of injury but traffic ceased and there was no income. Mr Robert Hughes of Ely House was instrumental in getting the bridge repaired on that occasion, perhaps because without it he had to travel around via Castlebridge and Ferrycarrig to get to town. As part of the repair job stone causeways were erected at either end thus reducing the wooden structure, thought to be dangerous. In fact the remedy nearly finished the bridge. Narrowing the river caused a stronger flow, which needed more expenditure on the bridge. You may still see the abutment at Ferrybank a few metres from the current bridge.

There were calls for the end of the tolls and eventually the Grand Jury – a forerunner of the County Council purchased the rights of the bridge from the shareholders for £10,000.00. Taking into account the income from the tolls over 50 years this had certainly proved to be a good investment. Opening the bridge in this way increased traffic. The bridge's popularity would lead to its downfall. Traffic became too much for it and in the 1850s a plan was unveiled for a new bridge. As a tragic footnote, many of those who were the original shareholders on the Oak Bridge at Wexford were executed there in the insurrection of 1798.

This 'new' bridge was built at Carcur, north of the town and linked to the Crosstown area. To confuse matters if you talk to Wexford people about this bridge today they will call it The Old Bridge although only the abutments remain.

The story is that the local Pierce Engineering firm built this bridge. The truth or otherwise of this statement is hard to establish. We can state that the company – renowned for over a century for its iron works and machinery manufacture – did produce the railings for the bridge. These iron railings survived for decades after the destruction of the bridge and were to be seen along Redmond Road until recent years.

For many people alive today, the old bridge will be remembered with its old style traffic calming features. These were sets of two big barrels painted red and white with a plank going from one to the other. These sets were placed like a ski slalom course along the bridge to cause traffic to drive in a slow zigzag fashion. It is a pity that our primary recollection should be on the bridge in such a decrepit state. The calming was essential when we realise that the bridge dated from the era of the pedestrian, the horse and cart or maybe a stagecoach. As it was still used in the 1950s we must marvel at the capacity to accept the weight of the motorcar and I suppose its eventual nemesis the lorry.

Sadly for many Wexford families it is the hearse and funeral cars that will be the abiding memory. From 1892 when St Ibar's Cemetery in Crosstown opened most residents of the town became more frequent visitors over this 'bridge of sighs'. It did have less mournful connotations. It was a beautiful walk on a summer Sunday, even if a cemetery visit was the ultimate reason.

Today with the new bridge under an almost continuous traffic jam we wonder at the short-sighted decision not only to close and demolish that beautiful old bridge but also to allow building on the abutment.

What a marvellous and healthy option it could have been as a pedestrian bridge giving easy access to Crosstown and a circular walk over the old and new bridges

The Oak Bridge: This detail from a painting dated around 1812 shows the oak bridge build by Lemuel Fox with ships in full sail and a cavalry troop and a carriage crossing. This is a stylised depiction particularly in relation to the ships. They could not have been anchored with sails aloft. The street leading from the quay at the left would have been Anne Street.

from the 1960s. If it had been left standing and rebuilt we might have had a unique option of another outlet for the traffic today.

The present bridge was completed and officially opened in 1959. It was a major engineering feat of its time with a company from Holland undertaking the task. I recall that one of the chief engineers lived at the corner of South Main Street and King Street during the construction. The re-opening of the bridge in this location brought new life to the area of Castlebridge parish on the opposite side. For over a century that had been a dead-end with little reason for people to travel further than Crosstown or Knottown. The new bridge gave people of Wexford easier access to the reclaimed lands of Ardcavan and the seashore at Ferrybank. It also opened access to The Dairy Fields. These are now under the swimming pool and caravan park but in the late 1900s they were a renowned courting venue for the youth of the town.

An interesting point about our bridges is that Carcur appears to have been the sturdiest in that it operated continuously for about a hundred years. The present bridge had to be completely re-fitted in less than fifty years, being cut back to its piers and rebuilt a few years ago.

THE FORT AT ROSSLARE

In the history of Wexford especially around the time of Cromwell there are a number of references to the fort at Rosslare but because all trace of it has disappeared it is often just glossed over.

Rosslare Strand was generally referred to by Wexford people as simply Rosslare - as opposed to Rosslare Harbour. It lies about fifteen kilometres from town by road and slightly less by rail, because the railway line cuts across the south sloblands. In earlier days it was closer still when hundreds of Wexford residents had small boats and could sail across the bay. In fact at times the water might be only a few feet deep in the harbour.

Rosslare had two distinct sections, the village where the majority of houses were located and the burrow. The burrow is made up of a narrow strip of land – mainly sand – that extends roughly northwards and almost reaches the point of The Raven stretching in the opposite direction, leaving a narrow inlet to Wexford Harbour. The strategic importance of this point on the burrow was recognised by the Confederate forces in 1642. They concocted a plan for a fort to be erected there as protection for the town and harbour of Wexford. The importance of the town and harbour cannot be over emphasised. It was from here that privateers harried shipping on the Irish sea and in many ways probably contributed to the retribution to be exacted by Oliver Cromwell less than a decade later.

Carcur Bridge

Seven cannon guns were installed there, each pointing seaward. A resident garrison, under the command of Paul Turner was located there. A map of Ireland dated 1610 by Speed shows a lighthouse near the site of the later fort. The fort eventually extended over 750 acres. Houses were erected over time to accommodate the growing population. They started with 12 houses around a square. This is said to have had a cobble-stoned courtyard with a central flagstaff that soared 70 feet high. This was the focal point of the fortification. The houses had earthen floors covered with sand.

A frigate was usually moored close by as a further safety measure. The observation post on the highest sand dune of the peninsula offered panoramic views of the harbour. All approaching vessels were spotted and observed as they entered the harbour. Tradition named the dune The Hill of Sixty with the second highest sand dune called The Hill of Bull. The fort had two wooden wharves; a rocket house, a village pump and boathouse. It is estimated that 50 dwellings were eventually built.

When Cromwell arrived in Wexford in October 1649, he ordered a 'fleet of twenty sail' under his son-in-law Henry Ireton to attack and seize the Fort of Rosslare. Stormy weather prevented the seaward approach and he then dispatched a large force of horse and foot soldiers under Lieutenant General Michael Jones to besiege it by land.

End of a Bridge: This is the old Carcur Bridge in the final stages of demolition. The Wexford Boat Club is to the left of the abutment. Housing development now covers the land opposite the bridge.

The small garrison held out until their supply of ammunition was exhausted. Ultimately they made their way to the frigate that was still moored nearby and made a final stand against superior numbers. Jones took possession of the Fort and his troops rounded-up the wives and children left behind. Yet another of the many legends of that October in Wexford we are told that, 'despite their pleas and the heart-rending shrieks they were all massacred without mercy in a dreaded cavern that was known locally thereafter as 'Cromwell's Murder Hole.'

The Fort lay idle for some years after that assault. In 1654, it was decided that the Fort of Rosslare should be restored and used for the defence of the Kingdom. It was in such a context that it became a Marine Revenue Station and Custom House. Commander Warren took charge of the fort in the early 1800s. He was

Ferrycarrig Bridge: the mode of transport is single horsepower. The tower commemorating the Crimean War is in place. The road alignment is the old one that wove around the castle- how many of you noticed that? It also weaves right along the river on the other side. The near section of the bridge is timber, to allow boats with masts to pass through. (Lawrence Collection)

the first Catholic to hold office and established the first chapel there in the upper floor of a house at the southern corner of the Square. Use as revenue station and customs post did not require a large garrison and by 1870 more than half of the dwellings had fallen into disuse and disrepair. The population continued to decline as many people moved to the thriving port town of Wexford.

Miss Shanahan was the teacher at the fort but she too moved to Wexford town where she opened a private school in South Main Street. The old Fort like all old historic settlements continued to attract interest and curiosity. Many explored it at weekends and during the summer holidays as Rosslare continued to grow as a destination. Some people bought the vacant houses as summer homes.

In the latter years of its official occupation there were Revenue or Custom Officers located there as well as pilots and lifeboat men. The womenfolk were noted for the unusual 'Prawskeens' or aprons they wore. These were rectangular in shape and made of strong jute fibre.

The sea that had played a major role in the formation of the peninsula or burrow in earlier centuries was also primarily responsible for its ultimate demise.

Building work in Wexford and at Rosslare Harbour – facilitating the cross channel shipping changed the flow of the currents in the harbour. These changes eroded part of the peninsula.

In the winters of the early 1920s, gale force winds drove heavy waves across the peninsula. It was breached in two places. Further winter storms added to the destruction and by 1926 the extreme tip of The Burrow had been reduced to a wind-swept ridge. The lifeboat men could not operate from the site and were forced to seek the safety of the mainland for their wives and children. Pilot men Peter and Larry Furlong were the last to leave, settling down near Raven Point on the northern side of the harbour entrance.

Looking at the northern tip of The Burrow peninsula today one would never imagine that it was once the site of a thriving community that had major military, commercial and maritime importance for centuries. We read of vanished civilisations in far away places but we seldom consider how whole villages have come and gone on our own doorstep. It is a cautionary reminder that nature can and does build up and destroy at will, although sometimes the destruction is aided by society.

STAINT PATRICK'S DAY 1914

The inaugural celebration of Saint Patrick's Day as a national holiday and holyday in Wexford was full of interest and spectacle.

The decision had only been taken a few weeks previously but all the population were enthusiastic in taking their part. Decoration of houses, shops and streets were highly praised. Main Street was particularly striking with The Mechanic's Institute getting special mention, as did the National Club in Anne Street. On the quays, flags and banners floated gaily in the breeze, those on Saint Iberius Catholic Club being very attractive. On the Crescent, from Meaghar's Forge to Mr. Walsh's Timber yard, a series of flags emblematic of maritime art and commerce crossed the Harbour Commissioners offices. On shipping on the quays ' orange and green were blended with the Union Jack and our national flags fluttered side by side'.

The Faythe was conspicuous by the absence of almost any attempt at decoration. Perhaps this was due to its width causing a problem.

At an early hour, bands and contingents from the suburbs commenced to pour in and by one o'clock the town presented an animated appearance. Despite the huge crowds not the slightest semblance of anything in the nature of disorder or intemperance was seen throughout the day. 'This pleasing feature of the day was to a great extent due to the generous action of the publicans of the town who almost to a man, consented to close their premises for the day'. Other businesses and manufactories also closed for the day.

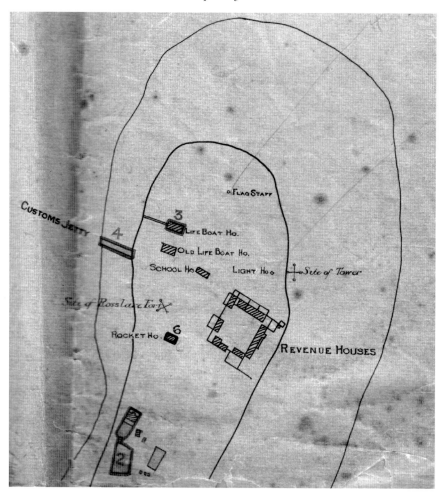

CUSTOMS JETTY

FLAG STAFF

3
LIFE BOAT HO.

4

OLD LIFE BOAT HO.

SCHOOL HO   LIGHT HO   Site of Tower

Site of Rosslare Fort

ROCKET HO.   6

REVENUE HOUSES

2

The Fort: This is a fragment of a map depicting part of the Rosslare Fort settlement.

The parade assembled at SaintPeter's Square. Punctually at two o'clock the Mayor, in chains of office and robes arrived, attended by his civic officers in their attractive regalia. His Worship was accompanied in his carriage by 'Wexford's Grand Old Man' Ben Hughes.

Saint Brigid's Fife and Drum Band led the procession along Joseph Street followed by members of the boy's branch of the Confraternity with their famous football club, The Blues and Whites. The Boys Brigade was marshalled by Fr. J. W. O'Byrne and was followed by Gaelic Leaguers from Wexford, Castlebridge and Crossabeg. With the mayor's carriage was the Enniscorthy Workingmen's Brass Band. Eighty members of the Kruger Club followed as well as a deputation from the Wexford '98 Borough Association. The Mechanics Institute had 200 members marching while the CYMS (St Iberius Club) fielded 150.

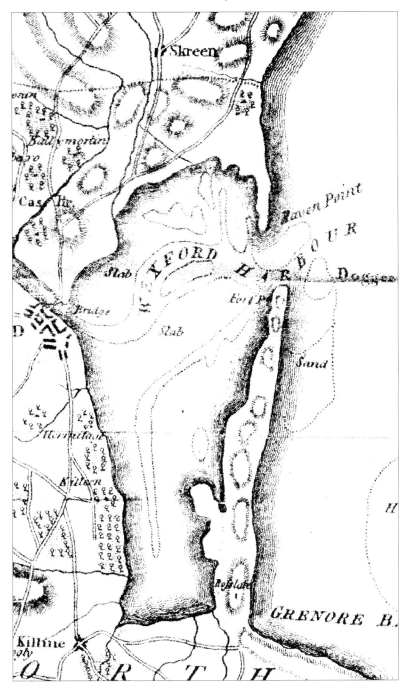

The Harbour: This old map clearly shows the Raven – subject of our poem – and The Rosslare Fort on the opposite peninsula.

'The little pupils of the Christian Brothers Schools numbered a couple of hundred and it was a sight to admire to see the order which the mites maintained and the manly manner in which the muscular little ones accomplished the rather long march.' Bridgetown and Blackwater bands accompanied them and were followed by the ironworkers of Doyle's, Pierce's and The Star foundries who made an imposing 'turn out'. The sailors were also involved under Captain Brady as were the carpenters, tailors and other trades.

The large group paraded through the town and returned to Saint Peter's Square where thee huge crowd was addressed by Fr. Cloney. At the end of his speech he urged the crowd, 'Drink not a drop of intoxicating liquor this holyday. Drowning the shamrock is a crime; it is a desecration of the day. Disband in peace, go home to your wives, your fathers and mothers, sisters and brothers.'

WORDS AND EXPRESSIONS

Throughout the centuries, Ireland has been renowned for it's contribution to learning and literature.

Our writers like Joyce and Wilde have given the English language more than a fair share of words and expressions. But on Wexford streets, many similarly important sayings were coined, adapted and most often stolen from other lands. Our mariners, sailing the oceans brought home foreign words and phrases, Wexfordmen serving in distant lands also imported new words.

Looking through older publications, listening to older people and recalling your own childhood, you may recall some of these words. Very few of these words can be claimed as exclusive to our area but all are or have been used in conversation in Wexford over a long period.

After in Wexford means 'later' as in 'I'll do it after'. This is a contraction of I'll do it after I do this.

Angish means sickly an in the phrase 'She's very angish looking'. It comes from the Yola language of Forth and Bargy that is a form of old English dating back to the time of Chaucer.

Any joy is our way of asking if there is any news. It probably derives from US Forces slang for 'good news'.

Back means to bet on as in 'he went to back a horse'. It probably comes from the idea of betting on something in the context of giving backing as in investing.

Bags is used to denote a mess as in 'He made a bags of it'.

Saint Patrick's Day Parade: This recalls the 1970s when our parades actually proceeded along the Main Street. The float is for Marechal Tents who had a factory in Kerlogue. (Rossiter Collection)

Parade: The building on the corner in mid picture is The Ritz Café where people sampled the produce of Frank O'Connor's Bakery. If memory serves me the Ladies Hair Fashions were by P.J. Doran. The Pye sign was over TVRS where we bought our records. (Rossiter Collection)

Bamped is used to denote blowing a car horn. The phrase, 'he bamped at her' is common.

Bardog is a type of small fish. It is often used as a nickname for people called Roche. This may come about though confusion with another small fish called a Roacheen, which could be translated as a small roach, hence bardog for a young Roche.

Baw ways denotes crooked as in 'he hammered the nail on baways'.

Blow in is any non-native of an area. Although common in Wexford it is descriptive slang from Australia circa 1942.

Bockety is another term for crooked as in 'it's a bockety table'.

Bow is the common Wexford term for the banshee. The word comes from Bugh a fairy queen of the Tuatha De Danann, the mythical Irish tribe

Bowsie is a guttersnipe or disreputable person, usually male. It probably derives from 'boozey' as in drunk.

Box means a blow for example one might say, 'he got a box in the forehead'. It comes from the Danish 'baske' meaning slap.

Brudge is a common mispronunciation of bridge

Caibosh is used in reference to having a detrimental effect on something, usually an event or action. The usage might be that 'he put the caibosh on it'.

Canat is a young trickster or troublemaker. Common usage would include 'he was just a little canat'.

Chaney alley was our reference to a type of playing marble. It probably comes from a corruption of china as in glazed pottery that they resemble..

Child sometimes meant specifically a girl as in the phrase 'Is it a boy or a child?'.

Chrissnen is an odd corruption of crescent. It is most common when referring to Crescent Quay in Wexford).

Clock was the name for black beetle. A superstition was that it caused rain if you killed one.

Cod is to fool or deceive. It may be related to the codpiece of earlier times that was used to deceive or exagerrate.

Codology is foolishness. The slang dates from 1910 and comes about from putting 'ology' at the end in mocking imitation of psychology etc.

Comeallye is used to denote a ballad or over popular song. It comes from the most common first line of many such songs as in 'Come all ye...'. It is also used as a derogatory term for some songs.

Cop on means to get some common sense as in 'cop onto yourself'. It comes from 'cope with'.

Court can be a friendly person of the opposite sex or the act of being extra friendly with such a person. In the former the phrase might be 'she was a great court' and in the latter,' he was determined to court her'. It comes from to court meaning to find favour with.

Cowslick was a very common reference a piece of hair that stuck out and was difficult to tame even with hair oil or cream. It was commented in the Book of the Dun Cow about Cuchulain

Crab was a contrary person. It could come from the sour juice of crab apples or the sideways gait of the crab.

Cranky meant bad tempered. It comes from the Anglo Saxon cranc meaning sick

Crator is a corruption poor creature and usually refers to an unfortunate person.

Craw meant the chest and was most commonly used as in ' he was a right crawthumper' usually meaning a hypocrite, especially in a religious sense. The word comes from the name of the first stomach of a fowl

Cut was our name for a lovely cake usually made up of leftovers. The proper name is a Chester Cake. The expression probably came about by the original cake as a large slab from which customers bought 'cuts' or portions.

Deadly meant great as in 'she looked deadly'. The origin is from 'dead on' as in dead on target

Deish meant lovely – 'She looked deish in her new coat'. It comes from the Gaelic 'deas' for nice.

Dekko meant a look or glance, 'Give us a dekko at the picture'. It is derived from the Romany 'dekho' to see.

Ditch is a built up boundary. Curiously it has the direct opposite meaning in England where it means a hole or trench.

Dull meant stupid, mad or insane.

Feck in one context is to fool as in 'to feck about'.

Feck in another context is to steal as in 'he fecked the pen'.

Feck was also used as an alternative to a similar swear word.

Fecker was a blackguard, again using as an alternative by changing one letter.

Feckin' was often used as an affirmative adjective as in 'you're feckin' right'.

Fetch meant a double or an apparition such as a ghost. It may derive from to recall or fetch back.

Figary meant a notion for example, 'he took a sudden figary to go down the field'. It comes from vagary to wander from whence we also get vagrant.

Fillums was a common pronunciation for films.

Furt meant a blow as in, 'he got a furt in the back'.

Get was a trickster. It might also be pronounced as git, a word more common elsewhere.

Grand meant fine e.g. 'I'm grand' as in splendid.

Great meant friendly. 'He's great with the Murphys'.

Heft was weight. You might be invited to 'get a heft of that'. It probably comes from heave

Hoeboy was a trickster.

Hop (on the) meant playing truant. It may derive from hop as an alternative to skip.

Hoult could refer to a fine body for example 'she was a fine hoult'. It may be a corruption of hold.

Jujus were almost any fruit jelly sweets. Some were said to resemble the fruit of the jujube tree.

Lard might mean good in the sense of, 'I'll beat the lard out of you'.

Lip meant to pout as in 'he had a lip on him.'

Minerals was the generic name for soft drinks with the phrase, 'Give us a bottle of minerals for the young fella.'

Mitch was another name for playing truant

Peg was a reference to throwing – 'he went to peg stones at the dog'. It is Australian slang *c*. 1930.

Piazz was once a common reference to The Bullring recalling the foreign sailors coming to the port who saw a resemblance to the piazza of their homeland.

Pictures was our reference to cinema –'we went to the pictures'.

Pismire was used to denote an ant, most often the winged ant.

Rack was a large toothed comb and probably came from rake.

Rantan meant having a spree – 'He was out on the rantan.' It originated from the German ranten meaning to move noisily.

Roacheens were small fish probably originally referring to young roach.

Rounds as in 'rounds of bread' was very common in Wexford. It referred to the whole slice.

Scootch meant either a ride or to shuffle along. You could say 'He got a scootch on the bike' or 'She scootched along the seat'. It may originate from boat-like boots used to move on sloblands or wetlands.

Scratch was the cheapest seats in an auditorium. It possibly implying flea ridden.

Shagged could mean threw as in 'he shagged him into the car'.

Shagged could also mean tired as in 'I was shagged after running down the road'.

Sniving meant full of as in 'the place was sniving with blackberries'. In an original context referring to a lake or river full of fish it might derive from the Gaelic snamh meaning to swim.

Soft referring to a child or baby meant young or immature.

Sprong is a Wexford for a garden fork. Could it arise from the S being in the wrong place on prongs?

Swing Swong was a swing for instance, 'the children played on the swing swong.'

Taped meant sized up as in 'she had him taped'. It possibly comes from measuring tape?

Taws meant marbles – 'we played taws after school'.

Terrible was very as in 'he was terrible nice'.

Turk could mean angry or annoyed as part of the phrase – 'she turned Turk'. It may have maritime origins if Wexford sailors did not get on with Turkish people on voyages to places like The Black Sea.

Twigged meant to figure out. 'I soon twigged to him.' It comes from the Gaelic tuig to understand.

Wainscotting in Wexford meant timber panels going halfway up an interior wall in a room or most often the entrance hall of a house.

Wash was the name for left over foods that was collected for feeding to pigs

Yez was the plural of you as in 'where are yez going?' Youse might also be used.

South Main Street: the position is determined by Sinnotts at number 29 according to their board with the key advertising the ironmongery warehouse. Directly opposite Sinnott's is a shop called Hoare – an unusual spelling for Wexford. Next door to that is a boot shop with wares hanging outside. The street is still rough. (Lawrence Collection)

Green Street: this picture gives a great feeling of the Wexford of around 1900. There is a mixture of whitewashed, thatched cottages and more urban two-storey slated dwellings. Some of the thatched houses have upper floors with 'dormer' windows barely visible. The sides of the street are cobbled to divert the water. The CBS School is still in The Faythe but the monastery is in place. The houses appear to be in excellent condition apart from one mid way down on the right. A small sign on one of the whitewashed houses advertises 'teas' so it is probably the local 'huckster shop'. (Lawrence Collection)

X

Citizens

Every town is filled with characters some of whose lives influenced the development of the area, others were interesting beings and most were just ordinary citizens.

To take on research of all such lives would fill a hundred volumes and more, a task beyond our resources. But because people make a town, we include a very short selection of mini-biographies.

NEWSPAPER MAN & POLITICIAN

John Greene was born in Wexford in 1803 and educated at the Diocesan School in Spawell Road along with James Roche later to become Reverend Roche and JT Devereux.

He was apprenticed to William Lord printer of *The Wexford Journal*. On completing his apprenticeship he left Wexford in 1828 and settled in Carlow where he founded a newspaper. He returned to Wexford some years later and founded *The Independent* supported by the local Liberal Party branch. As the proprietor and editor he was prosecuted and jailed for anti-tithe articles. In 1840 he was elected to the Corporation and represented Selskar Ward for 50 years during which he was mayor on seven occasions. Greene was a champion of piped water supplies for the town. He supported O'Connell and opposed Parnell. John Greene was a justice of the peace and Deputy Lieutenant of the county but declined a knighthood. He was married to Mary Sweetman and had four sons, two of whom became barristers, one a priest and the other a doctor. John Greene died in 1890.

DOCTOR HADDEN

George Hadden was born in Wexford but spent his early years studying abroad.

With his wife, Helen, he then worked as a missionary doctor in both China and Siberia. Returning to Wexford in the 1930s he entered fully into the political and social life of his native town. As well as being involved in the Boat Club and the Cage Bird Society, Dr. Hadden was founder member of two organizations that became Wexford institutions. One was the Wexford Male Voice Choir and the other Wexford Historical Society or as it was originally called The Old Wexford Society. The good doctor who can still be remembered striding along our streets with white hair, flowing beard and a long staff was also elected to Wexford Corporation. He was made a freeman of the borough in 1972. He wrote and lectured widely on our heritage up until his death in 1973 at the age of 91 years.

THE SCHOLAR POET

PR Hanrahan was born in Wexford and acted as principal of the Lancastrian School, in School Street in the premises now called Lancaster House, from 1831 until it was disestablished in 1878.

Like many a schoolmaster of that era, he was a classical scholar and he loved poetry. A collection of his work was published as *Echoes of the Past*. This volume included *The Fetch*. The poem had a supernatural theme with the following lines reflecting a forgotten part of our folklore:

'I knew he'd die
For the banshee's song
The whole night long
Was heard from the bawn..
I knew he'd die
For the fetch was seen
In the green boreen
By the fairy's path'

Mr. Hanrahan died at Farnogue Cottage aged 78 and he is buried at Carrig.

THE EXPLORER

Robert McClure was born on North Main Street in Wexford, in a house that would later be incorporated into the old White's Hotel, on 28 January 1807.

He was the son of a naval officer. At an early age he went to Sandhurst, the military school in England. From there he joined the navy and served on Nelson's 'Victory'. But it is for exploration rather than fighting this son of Wexford is best remembered. On the ship called 'The Investigator' he was among the crew that discovered the north west passage allowing ships to sail around the north coast of the Americas. McClure was knighted for his efforts. He died in London in 1873.

BLACK LEAD

Black Lead 'appeared' in South Wexford, in the months following the First World War.

He was a rather sinister looking character with long hair and beard. His hat was always bent like a souwester. He carried a bag like a sporran held around his neck by a string. To add to the mystery he covered himself, his clothes and bag in the substance that gave him his name — black lead. During his time in Wexford he is said never to have named himself or professed any religion.

He was said to have spoken several languages and showed great manners and gently begged for alms. He always said 'God bless you?' and gently looked at you as if it was a combined responsibility and privilege to support him in frugal comfort. He lived for some time in one of the houses owned by the late Mrs. Katherine Scallan of Drinagh. Occasionally, he resided in the grandly titled, The Shelbourne Hotel at Cornmarket or as it was occasionally known, 'The Flying Flea' where many men of the road lodged. Think of the song 'Louse House in Kilkenny'. There is a tradition that he went for a swim every day of the year in the canal of the South Slob.

He was a harmless character who attracted affection as he roamed the roads, but maintaining a perpetual cloud of secrecy. No one ever knew his name, and looking at a picture of him one would seem to need great courage to ask him directly.

It is said that he called for the priest in his final hours and was attended by Fr. Michael O'Neill and local lore states that he left between £300 and £600 in cash for charitable purposes in Wexford. He carried his origins, his profession and the secret of his life previous to his arrival in Wexford, with him to the grave.

He may well have been one of the millions of victims of the terrible First World War, at a time when shell-shocked wanderers abounded. We will never know what brought him to our town. Because he stayed in County Wexford we must assume he was contented and at peace here.

LAST OF THE WEXFORD SAIL MAKERS

Sometimes it is by looking at the life of a single individual we are made aware of the diversity of talents and accomplishments that exist in a small town.

If we even take a great-uncle of mine who died a few years ago we are reminded of this. James Walsh, 5 Saint Columba's Villas, Wexford was the last person to carry on the famous Wexford tradition of sail making. He was a son of the late Mr. and Mrs. John Walsh of William Street and a member of a family that had strong connections with the maritime life of the town stretching back over many decades.

He was one of the last remaining Wexfordmen who could boast having sailed out of the port on the famous sail borne clipper ships, but it was as a sail maker with few peers that he made his reputation. He learned the art from his father and uncle and in a career spanning more than fifty years, fitted out all types of craft. A man of many talents, Mr. Walsh was also a keen yachtsman and won numerous races in regattas over the years particularly with the skiff, 'Fair Do', owned by his brother, John of William Street.

A supremely skilled craftsman, Mr. Walsh had also worked for the old Wexford firm of Lamberts, coach-smiths and boat builders and in the blacksmith's forge of Pierces foundry He spent some time serving with the Irish Lights and for many years his talents were in' constant demand in the making of lorry covers and repairs to all types of canvas

With life-long friend, Eddie O'Brien of Hill Street, Mr. Walsh was a pioneer of the mussel fishing industry in Wexford. Both men were amongst the first to fish for mussels in Wexford Harbour for the Lett family that went on to open worldwide markets for the product. In 1922 when bombs damaged Wexford Bridge during the Civil War, Mr. Walsh, his brother Tom and uncle Edward, provided a ferry service across the River Slaney for funerals to Crosstown Cemetery.

WEXFORD, THE DAY BEFORE PRESIDENT KENNEDY'S VISIT.

The Day Before: Such was the excitement of the visit of John F. Kennedy that this special postcard was on sale showing Wexford in June 1963. The ladies in Abbey Street are washing the windows. A couple of lads are heading down to The Crescent. The trawler men are busy. South Main Street is bedecked with bunting. (Wexford Library Collection)

North Main Street: The in picture caption is wrong. On the left is the office of *The Wexford Independent*.

Visit of the prince Royal of Arabia (Faisal Ibn Saud) and Suite to Wexford Sunday November 9 1919. Photo taken at Mr MJ O'Connor's Shooting Lodge, North Slob Wexford by Vize of Wexford. (O'Connor Collection)

Main Street

Towards the Tholsel

MJ O'Connors: This fine red brick building housed the firm of solicitors for decades.
(O'Connor Collection)

North Main Street (O'Connor Collection)